Wood Knocks:

Journal of Sasquatch Research

VOLUME III

Wood Knocks:
Journal of Sasquatch Research
VOLUME III

by David Weatherly

Leprechaun Press
NEVADA

Wood Knocks:
Journal of Sasquatch Research
VOLUME III
by David Weatherly

ISBN: 978-1-945950-06-3 (Paperback)

Published by:

Leprechaun Productions
Nevada

Cover by: Sam Shearon
www.mister-sam.com

Edited by: A. Dale Triplett
@DaleTriplett

Interior design by: SMAK
www.smakgraphics.com

Printed in the United States of America

Author's Introduction

Welcome to the third volume of Wood Knocks: Journal of Sasquatch Research. As with previous volumes, you'll find an array of views and opinions on the mysterious hairy creature known as Bigfoot. And this time, some truly unique articles grace the pages.

Timothy Renner's article opens in 1886 and covers some fascinating historical accounts from Pennsylvania. "The Company They Keep" is a fitting title, since it seems the residents of the northern state have been living with strange creatures since the early days of settlement.

My own contribution this volume addresses Bigfoot encounters in Arizona. Known for the Grand Canyon and beautiful, panoramic views, Arizona also has forest, mountains and a lot of sparsely populated land. Land that may be a refuge for something as yet unidentified by scientists but accepted as real by the original Native American inhabitants of the region.

It's always great to have an article from the prolific Nick Redfern, and he doesn't disappoint with "The "Demon" Bigfoot of the U.K." Who could resist a thorough reading with a title like that?

Floridian Robert Robinson comes in this volume with an article on the Skunk Ape. The Sunshine state is rich in wildlife and resources and of course, it's home to the Everglades, a large, watery expanse that's both beautiful and dangerous. Florida may be a haven for vacationers and retirees, but as Robinson explains, it may also be the refuge of the Skunk Ape.

Marvin Leeper may not be a familiar voice to some of you, but his excellent study of Bigfoot in Oklahoma will make you stand up and pay attention. Leeper covers a lot of ground for a state that doesn't get as much attention from researchers as its southern neighbor, Texas. Oklahoma, though, is a real hotbed of activity and the amount of research Leeper has done is impressive.

Stone throwing, whistling and foul odors are only a couple of the things that fortean author Joshua Cutchin addresses in his contribution. Cutchin has been collecting an amazing amount of data for his forays into various strange topics and here he delves into some of the lesser addressed anomalies involving the hairy creatures.

Bruce Champagne weighs in with one of my favorite topics in the field, a study of Sasquatch in the desert. While many people have a hard time believing that large, bipedal creatures are roaming around the desert states, Champagne comes in with some great evidence and presents the potential of their existence along with scientific analysis of their presence in dry climates.

Finally, thanks to the stunning talents of cover artist Sam Shearon for another great depiction of Sasquatch, the skill of layout and design master SMAK and editor Dale Triplett for making sure all the I's are dotted and T's are crossed.

So grab some coffee and set aside some time, there's a lot to ponder as we delve once again into the cryptozoological world of Sasquatch.

Enjoy!

- David Weatherly

Table of Contents

Arizona's Mysterious Deserts (photo by author)

Bigfoot in Arizona

by David Weatherly

Arizona is the sixth largest state in the United States. Lying in the beautiful southwest region of the country, it ranks 14th in population. Arizona is one of the "four corners," where the four states of Arizona, Utah, New Mexico and Colorado meet at a singular point.

Arizona was the last of the contiguous states to be admitted to the Union, gaining statehood in 1912. Almost one quarter of the state is made up of Native American Reservations, home to 27 federally recognized tribes, including the Navajo Nation, the largest reservation in the country. Only about 15% of the land in Arizona is privately owned, with the remainder being park land, public forest and Native American reservations.

While most people perceive the state as being dry, arid and covered with cacti and desert, the landscape is actually very diverse. While it's true much of the southern portion of the state is desert, the northern portion is rich in forests and mountain ranges. There are several national forests and parks, and the state is home to the magnificent Grand Canyon National Park, one of the designated "Seven Natural Wonders of the World."

One geographical feature of note is the Mogollon Rim, a 1,998-foot escarpment that cuts through the central portion of the state and marks the southwestern edge of the Colorado Plateau.

The state is home to one of the most well-preserved meteorite impact sites in the world, as well as ski resorts, popular tourist destinations, and historic, old West ghost towns like Tombstone.

It may also be home to a monster.

A monster so well known that Arizona's official balladeer, Dolan Ellis, included it in a song written as part of an anti-littering campaign back in 1966.

The Mogollon Monster

The Mogollon Rim is a topographical/geological feature that extends for approximately 200 miles across Arizona. Starting in northern Yavapai County, the rim runs eastward and ends near the state's border with New Mexico. The rim forms the southern edge of the Colorado Plateau.

The Mogollon Rim was named after Don Juan Ignacio Flores Mogollon, Spanish Governor of New Mexico from 1712 to 1715. The escarpment includes high cliffs of sandstone and limestone, dramatic canyons including Pine Canyon and Fossil Creek, and numerous sources of fresh water. Extensive forests of ponderosa pine cover the rim's slopes.

Most of the Mogollon Rim is at four to five thousand feet in elevation, with its highest point reaching to about eight thousand feet. The region is a prime habitat for a wide range of wildlife including elk, bighorn sheep, antelope, wild turkeys and even mountain lions. The Mexican gray wolf was also recently reintroduced to the region.

A massive wildfire devastated part of the rim in 2002. On record as Arizona's second largest wildfire, the "Rodeo-Chediski" fire burned 469,000 acres and 426 structures. The destruction was massive.

The Mogollon Rim is partially bisected by Interstate 17 which runs north to south between Flagstaff and Phoenix. Towns that lie near the rim include Sedona, Payson, Show Low and Alpine.

Both the rim itself, and the towns around it, have often been a focal point of Bigfoot sightings. In fact, there have been so many encounters through the years that the creature has a regional nickname, "The Mogollon Monster."

In general, the monster is described as a bipedal humanoid around seven to eight feet tall. Its eyes are reportedly red and much of its body is covered in long black or reddish-brown hair. Many reports claim the creature has a strong pungent odor variously described as "dead fish," "rotting meat," or"extremely bad body odor."

There are recorded sightings of a large, hairy creature that predate the name, but once the fanciful moniker was applied, it stuck, and now most sightings in the region are dubbed encounters with the Mogollon Monster.

The nickname seems to have been derived from a campfire story told by the Boy Scouts of America. Numerous men who spent time in Arizona as scouts recall the story, but it has several variations. The tales are centered around Camp Geronimo. The site is a year round camp, located north of Payson. It's a scenic, wilderness location described by the official Website as:

"...located north of Payson in the shadows of the magnificent Mogollon Rim on nearly 200 acres of forest and meadows.

Surrounded by over 5,000 acres of ponderosa pine forest, trails lead from Camp Geronimo to the top of the rim where Scouts can stand at the very edge of the Colorado Plateau."

The site is a prime location for creepy stories by the fireside, and scouts who visit the camp have a long tradition of telling tales of the Mogollon Monster.

In one version of the story, the creature was said to have attacked the camp and caused death and destruction, destroying everything in its path in a fit of rage.

Another version involves Arizona pioneer Sam Spade who built a log cabin on land adjacent to what is now the camp. Spade was purportedly attacked by the creature and suffered a mental breakdown as a result of the encounter. Later, Spade's son and fiancé were supposedly killed by the creature on their wedding day.

Other versions of the Mogollon monster campfire story involve a native chief who transformed into the creature, and a white man damned by native spirits to wander the forests.

As the name implies, most sightings of the Mogollon Monster occur in and around the Rim country. The giant biped's territory purportedly covers an area that stretches from Prescott to Williams in the north, east to Winslow and south to Heber.

Apache and Navajo legends in the region speak of the "Big Hairy

Man," or "The Old Man of the Mountain," and go back hundreds of years. There are also sightings that stretch back decades from ranchers and cowboys, forestry workers and outdoorsmen.

While most accounts fall within the standard fare of Bigfoot sightings, a fair percentage of people who spot the creature say it's aggressive, territorial and sometimes even violent. Researchers in the region state the monster often throws rocks and heavy tree limbs to frighten intruders. Primarily nocturnal, the creature will enter campsites and raid provisions when the opportunity presents itself.

Other witnesses claim they've heard a "blood-curdling" scream unlike any known animal, and an eerie silence falls over the area just before the creature appears.

The earliest recorded account of an encounter with the creature appears to be from a 1903 edition of *The Arizona Republican.*The paper printed a report in which a man named I.W. Stevens described a creature he saw near the Grand Canyon. According to Stevens, the creature had:

"...long white hair and matted beard that reached to his knees. It wore no clothing, and upon his talon like fingers were claws at least two inches long. A coat of gray hair nearly covered his body, with here and there a spot of dirty skin showing."

Stevens claimed he came upon the wild man as it sat perched on rocks near the water. He also watched as the creature drank the blood of two dead cougars. Stevens, who was in a boat at the time, was sickened by the sight:

"I stood up in the boat and yelled. The man sprang to his feet, took a long look at me, and then fled up from a ledge...here he flourished his club again and screamed the wildest, most unearthly screech I ever heard then turned and sprang up the craggy wall of the canyon...I packed my outfit into the boat and drifted down and out of the canyon before I made camp for the night. That was the strangest adventure of my life."

While it's certainly true that papers of the period often ran questionable stories, there's no denying tales of the monster have a long history along the rim. Modern reports range from Prescott in the north, to Williams in the southeast, to Alpine and Clifton.

Cryptozoologist Don Davis, who passed away in 2002, claimed to have seen the monster himself in the 1940s. Davis was a boy scout and was spending time at Camp Geronimo. Davis described the creature in his account:

"The creature was huge. Its eyes were deep set and hard to see, but they seemed expressionless. His face seemed pretty much devoid of hair, but there seemed to be hair along the sides of his face. His chest, shoulders and arms were massive, especially the upper arms; easily upwards of 6 inches in diameter, perhaps much, much more. I could see he was pretty hairy but didn't observe really how thick the body hair was. The face/ head was very square; square sides and squared up chin, like a box."

In 1990, blogger Ken Hulsey had a strange encounter on AZ highway 180. He later shared details of the encounter on the Cryptomundo Website.

Hulsey was on a road trip from California, back to his home in New Mexico. A girlfriend was with him and they stopped off for a detour to see the Grand Canyon. After some sightseeing, the couple hit the road again, cutting across on Highway 180, heading for I-40 and Flagstaff. Hulsey was driving at a normal pace. As he recalls:

"The trip started out normal enough. Just a typical drive through the mountains. There were few cars on the highway that evening, as I remember it, and the road was kinda curvy—winding through the mountains. By this time the sun had set, and it was getting dark.

This is when it happened.

I remember coming around a curve in the highway and there was a long straight-away in front of us before the road turned again.

As we began to proceed down the straight section, we both noticed a very large animal walking down the right side of the road. Since I had just came out of a curve, the car wasn't moving very fast, and when I saw the animal, I slowed the car even further."

The couple was stunned at the sight. Hulsey's companion spoke out loud, wondering if they were seeing a bear, but they quickly realized it was something they'd never seen before.

"As we came closer to the animal, it became apparent quickly that what we were looking at was not a bear. There was a very large, hairy mass walking away from us on two legs. I can still remember the arms swaying as it strolled naturally down the side of the road away from us.

As we got closer, about 50 yards or more as I remember it, the car's headlights shown past the creature. It was at that time that our companion on the highway became aware of our presence. It stopped, and I stopped."

The couple tried to wrap their minds around what they were seeing. Hulsey's companion became frightened at the sight, while he himself tried to reconcile the creature's presence. Their encounter became even more unusual because the creature didn't just dart off out of sight as is often the case in Bigfoot sightings. Instead, it became curious about the vehicle.

"I remember this vividly; the animal went to turn around to get a look at us. Now this was odd, because the animal had no neck, or not much of one, so it couldn't turn its head to look at us, it had to turn its whole upper body.

That apparently wasn't good enough for the creature, so it turned around completely to face us.

What was there before us was this giant...well, ape. It was about seven to eight feet tall (about the same height as a road sign to my estimation), covered in brown fur, large...with very little definition. That is to say that it didn't have a typical human build. Kinda built like a 'brick wall,' like a football lineman, large from head to toe."

Hulsey recalls the animal resembled a character from "Planet of the Apes," with areas on the face that appeared hairless, especially around the mouth, nose and eyes. He recalls the eyes being cat-like, with a reflection of green from the vehicle's headlights.

"The animal was covered in very 'shaggy' fur, possibly an inch or more in length. On the arms the hair was twice as long, or so, than it was on the head and body. The color was mostly a chocolate brown color, but I remember there being lighter spots in some areas."

Hulsey writes that as he observed the Bigfoot, he could tell it was curious about the vehicle. As he watched, the creature "rubbed its tongue across its front teeth," a gesture Hulsey interpreted as a sign of curiosity as it calculated its next move.

That move was to take a couple of strides towards the vehicle. Hulsey's passenger panicked and started screaming, believing the creature was going to attack. The noise caused the Bigfoot to stop its approach, turn, and take two long strides off into the trees on the side of the road.

In a flash, the creature had vanished.

"My girlfriend stopped her panic attack and we sat there silently looking at the spot where the creature once stood. I think we sat there for some time before I snapped out of my trance and decided to get out of there in case the Bigfoot came back.

I remember driving onto the left-hand side of the road, just in case the creature came charging out of the woods at us or something.

We looked into the woods as we drove past the spot where it had been and saw nothing.

Amazingly, after we had gotten back on I-40 in Flagstaff, we both acted as if nothing had happened."

Hulsey and the woman soon split, and he kept quiet about the encounter for several years. It wasn't until 2005 that he submitted his account to the BFRO and other websites.

Cryptozoologists Join the Hunt

Cryptozoologist Mitchell Waite did extensive research on the Mogollon monster, and for a time ran the Mogollon monster Website. Sadly, Waite passed away in April of 2015. Waite gathered video and photographic evidence, as well as casts of footprints and other physical evidence. He was a consummate outdoorsman and spent a lot of time working the field and having experiences. He was a great asset to the field and is still missed.

Waite's research partner, Susan Farnsworth, has written a couple of books on Bigfoot in Arizona and has some interesting accounts. On the Mogollon monster Website, she detailed an encounter from 2008.

She and a fellow researcher, listed as "DR" in the report, were camping at an area near a well and spring. That night, Farnsworth was awoken:

"About 2:30 am I awoke to a very foul stench. It smelled like decomposing fish. It was very strong and was turning my stomach. I was laying on my back facing up when I opened my eyes. Instantly, I noticed the tent side was about two inches from my nose. I was terrified.

Something was actually pushing my side of the tent down on top of me."

Farnsworth writes that she located her pistol while calling out to wake DR. She then began to scream loudly, and events unfolded quickly.

DR rose quickly and began to make loud noises to frighten whatever was outside the tent. The pair turned on an electric lantern and pitched it outside to illuminate the area. After a few moments, they made their way out of the tent and to their truck, leaving the area and staying the night in a nearby town.

The next day, they returned to camp to gather their gear. They searched the area but could find no footprints. There was an area where pine needles had been pushed down and a large impression left. Unfortunately, they had not set up any motion detectors or trail cameras, so no photographic evidence was captured.

A week later, researcher Mitch Waite led an expedition back to the tent site to investigate further.

A thorough search by Waite and his team led to the discovery of several impressions that appeared to have been made by very large feet. What appeared to be bedding areas were also found with broken branches and leaves piled up under trees.

Making their way back to the main road, the investigators ran into a Forest Ranger and stopped for a conversation. The Ranger told the team that no bears had been reported in the area for at least two years. He also stated he had been finding scat in the area that he couldn't identify.

After the Ranger departed, the team discovered a massive footprint along the side of the road. It measured 19 inches in length, 9 inches through the ball of the foot, and 4 inches wide at the heel. A plaster cast was taken of the print.

Another Arizona cryptozoologist also searches for the monster. Alex Hearn runs AZCRO, the Arizona Cryptozoological Research Organization. The group focuses on regional cryptid mysteries and has pursued reports of the Mogollon monster for several years.

Hearn himself saw the creature in 2008, just off Highway 288, twenty miles south of Young. He recalls the sighting:

"He had reddish brown hair—the most unique thing that I saw. I

don't know if this means it's a female. It was very upright: I looked to my left and there was this brown head and shoulder, raising its arm up in almost a swimming motion, lifting the branches out of the way.

It had human-looking eyes—very dark and big. It did have a huge, huge brow—that seemed to be more brownish skin. The eyes were deep and stared right at me: I was caught in this glance. It didn't look away. Its eyebrows went up."

Hearn reported the creature was around seven feet tall. He collected both hair samples and a plaster cast of a footprint from the location.

Hearn hit the news in February 2013, when CBS 5 news, out of Phoenix, ran a story on his discovery of a toenail he believed came off one of the creatures. Hearn told reporters:

"Everybody has a desire to know the unexplained and to find the truth. The toenail is proof that the creature is there. But it's not the definitive proof yet, we still have work to do."

Hearn sent the toenail to a laboratory for DNA analysis. The results stated the sample was:

"A 100 percent human female, mixed with a male of an unknown species."

Hearn was satisfied the results proved the sample was from a Bigfoot and he isn't concerned about the skeptics:

"I don't try to persuade them. But I will show them the evidence that we found, they're welcome to come with us."

Tales of the Mogollon Monster even attracted the attention of Reality TV. Animal Planet's hit show, "Finding Bigfoot," showed up in Payson in March 2012 to look into sightings around the Rim. Show producers stated they received twenty accounts before the crew even arrived for the town hall meeting. One producer noted:

"We do our research before we come, we wouldn't come here if we didn't know there were a lot of sightings."

Gathered at Payson's Oxbow Saloon, cast and crew listened to numerous accounts of creature sightings scattered from Payson to Show Low and over into the White Mountains. Some accounts went as far back as the 1970s, while others were much more recent.

Payson—Monster Hotspot

The choice of Payson was an excellent one for the Finding Bigfoot show's starting point. Many researchers find the town to be an epicenter of encounters.

Located in Gila County, Payson is nicknamed "The Heart of Arizona," since it is near the geographical center of the state. With an elevation of almost 5,000 feet, the scenic town is surrounded by the Tonto National Forest and offers year round outdoor activities. The area has a Mediterranean climate, a population of just over 15,000... and maybe a few monsters.

The Payson area yields a lot of reports of the creatures crossing roads, perhaps because of the town's central location. A prime example is an account from 2006 that was reported to the BFRO.

On November 17th, the witness was driving on Highway 260 near Payson and hit a spot where the divided highway starts to head up to the Mogollon rim. The creature was spotted on the roadside.

"It was standing on the side of the road, as it if was waiting to cross. It was standing next to a large diamond road sign that I believe is about 7 feet tall. It was taller than the sign by a head, making it about 8 feet tall. It was illuminated by the side lights on my car, so I didn't see much definition in the face, but I saw a good outline of the head, and I saw a distinct large head that was not particularly pointed but was sloping. The shoulders were massive and boxy. The arms were long and hung down to the knees. It was light colored, almost the color of the oak leaves in the fall. The hair was short, about 3-4 inches long, and normal in distribution—it was not bushy. I say "it" because I didn't notice any anatomy."

An even stranger sighting from the area hit the Internet in 2014 from a woman who claimed the creature she saw looked like a "troll."

The account, reportedly from a twenty-eight-year-old woman in Payson, detailed an experience she had while hiking the rim's Canyon Point trail.

"Y. Estevez," says she was alone on the trail when she saw something kneeling down, drinking water:

"It was on its knees, drinking water, when I found it. Drinking, making noises like a pig, so at first sight the animal looked like a pig to me."

Estevez says she attempted to get out her camera, but the noise alerted the creature to her presence. The creature then rose up on two legs and she got a good look at it:

"It had long hair, grey and bluish, and I swear it looked like one of those trolls from a fairy tale. Ugly stuff. The face was human looking, no hair on it, but full of bumps. The eyes were kind of a brown-red. Thick big nose, small lips. No expression on its face at all. It then took off running like a person."

Eighteen miles north of Payson, the small town of Strawberry gets its share of monster reports too. An eyewitness in the area says he spotted the creature in the Coconino National Forest on June 26, 2016.

Camping in a USFS campground in the Mogollon Rim, the man states:

"I had finished reading a book when I looked across the campground and I noticed a very fast moving dark figure, heading from north to south.

It ran with a slight forward slant to its body. Its head did not bob up and down like a human runner's head at that speed."

When he first spotted the creature, the witness thought it was someone on a bike because the movement was so fast. He quickly realized he was seeing something far more unusual:

"It was a very large Bigfoot. It only lasted about three seconds, but I was lucky to see it at all.

It moved faster than a human could run."

The man said the creature's hair was almost black with a slight reddish tint. Due to the distance, about 125 yards, he was unable to see any facial details.

An investigator from the BFRO went to the scene and found impressions where the creature was spotted. The investigator was on site nine days after the incident, so an accurate measurement of the footprint's size could not be determined. Length of stride was calculated however and determined to be longer than a human could achieve.

Using points of reference at the location, the creature's height was estimated to be around eight feet.

Encounters in Central Arizona

In 1972, Fate magazine received details of an encounter from the Flagstaff area. Writing in the November issue, reader Mabel Fulcher of Yarnell, Arizona recounted her experiences from the 1920s:

"We first saw it in the late summer of 1924 at our ranch home at the foot of the San Francisco Peaks five miles northwest of Flagstaff, Ariz.

The garden had matured and there was an abundance of corn and other vegetables. My mother and I had started down to the garden which was about a quarter mile from the house. We were walking along halfway between the house and garden, when my mother looked up and saw what she thought was my husband. He always spent considerable time taking care of the garden. I looked too, but what I saw didn't look like my husband.

"It" had an armload of corn, and was bent over, pulling up turnips. My mother called, ran forward a little distance, then waved.

The "thing" stood up straight, and I figured it was about seven feet tall and weighed about 400 pounds. It was light in color and seemed to have a hairy body. Anyway, it seemed frightened and took off through the wheat field and jumped over the rail fence, disappearing in the thick forest of young pine trees.

Many times after that we would get a glimpse of something around the hay shed or barn and occasionally the farm animals would become frightened and stampede. We often missed a few chickens and turkeys but never really got a good look at "the thing" again in the years we lived there. However, at times there would be reports of someone seeing an "animal" running through the forest on two legs.

South of Flagstaff, in the beautiful town of Sedona, tourists flock to see the sacred sites, known as "vortexes," and indulge in a range of new age therapies.

Such things weren't on the mind of a trio of frog hunters who had a strange experience at Beaver Creek, in an area between Sedona and Rimrock.

It was June 29, 2014 when the group went out to the water. It was 12:40 A.M. and all the men had 100 lumen lights. They were walking upstream after entering a canyon to get to the creek. When they entered the canyon, the reporting witness says he noticed a "musky, stinky smell." The man tried to ignore the odor, thinking it was likely skunk or javelina, both common in the area.

"After walking for about 200 yards, my son who was in front stopped and said he heard something walking away from him up the creek. I asked if it was a deer or elk. He told me he could not see because of the underbrush, but said it sounded like a heavy person."

The trio continued on, but things took on a more threatening tone. As the witness recounts:

"We continued for a few more feet and we all then observed three large rocks thrown from the thick brush above our heads, about 20 yards in front of us over the creek to the opposite side. We all stopped and then heard branches crashing as something crossed the creek in front of us. We looked in all directions with our lights, but the brush and trees were too thick to see."

The trio also heard more branches being broken and another rock thrown at them, landing in the creek 5 yards in front of their position. They made their way out of the area.

In a follow up interview, the man stated the rocks were thrown from the top of a small vertical cliff about twenty feet from where they were at the time. Estimates of the rock's size put them at about the same as a softball.

The reporting witness in this case was a retired police officer and lifelong outdoorsman and hunter.

Historic Prescott yields numerous encounters too. Among them is another roadside sighting.

In August 1981, the witness was on the Thumb Butte Loop when he had this experience:

"I was on the Thumb Butte Loop in Prescott next to the city park. While driving I spotted a reddish-brown ape like creature. I stopped the car immediately and observed the creature. The hair on his arms was longer than the rest. It appeared to have little or no neck. It appeared to be very muscular and covered ground quickly. It was hard to judge the height of the creature because of the distance and shock but I knew it was tall. It walked in the tree line and there was a gap in the trees about 75 meters long. I watched this creature walk through the opening. I remember his arms swinging and he only looked forward. I estimated

(through military experience) that it was 100 meters from my position. I was sitting in the car with my head turned looking out the back and side window. I estimate that I saw him for at least 10 seconds although it seemed longer.

What I remember most is my mind was wrestling with the thought that what I was seeing was not supposed to exist, yet I was viewing it. It was a most unsettling experience."

Notes from a follow up investigation reveal that the creature's gait was "huge" and it traveled 75 meters "in no time." The side of the face visible to the witness was black and the creature's hands swung up close to shoulder height.

The man was driving on a dirt road toward Deering Park and the time was between six and seven p.m.

Further to the east, but still near the Mogollon Rim, is the small town of Show Low. The area is a popular recreation spot and sits at an elevation of 6,400 feet. Show Low is in Navajo County and is an area with extensive forests.

An encounter posted on the BFRO database recounts a sighting on US 60 that occurred March 24th, 2010. The witness writes:

"I was driving towards Show Low on US 60 about 2:00 in the afternoon on March 24th, 2010. I always look out into the trees in hopes of seeing deer and turkeys, but this time I saw something a bit out of the ordinary. I saw a very large and tall animal which was about the same reddish-brown color as a Hereford cow, standing about halfway behind a large pine tree. Its arm was very long, and it was probably 7ft or more in height. I hit the brakes and slowed way down to get a better look and when doing so, it rotated to make itself more hidden from view. It was too large for the tree it was behind, and now it was visible on both sides of the tree. It definitely saw me. I couldn't see its eyes, but it kept its head visible to look at me. Cars were coming so I had to move on."

The witness, a seasoned hunter, is very familiar with local wildlife and has driven the route on many occasions. He further described the creature as having a human-like shape with broad shoulders and muscular, bulky arms. No neck was visible, and the hair was dark red two to three inches in length. The man further noted the creature's arms hung down far below its waist and "did not hang straight as ours do but more like a gorilla's."

Another report I received from Show Low was from a witness who encountered a Sasquatch while he was taking a walk in the area in 2012.

The man and a friend were staying in the area and had started taking daily walks in the surrounding forest to take in the scenery and enjoy the fresh air. He was surprised to encounter something he never even considered really existed:

"My friend and I were taking a walk. It was about five o'clock in the afternoon. We heard an odd sound, sort of a low grumbling noise. It was very deep, not like a dog, but like something from a larger animal. We both stopped and started looking around to see what had made the noise. My friend spotted it first and pointed it out to me saying 'look!'

Over by some pine trees there was a tall creature, I'd say it was around seven feet tall or a little more. I couldn't really see facial features very well because it all happened so fast. The creature was brown in color and dirty looking. The hair was long all over the body. The shoulders were very broad, and it didn't really look like it had a neck at all, just bulky shoulders going straight into its head. It was on two legs and I knew right away it wasn't a bear or any other kind of animal that I had ever seen.

It looked at us and my first thought was this it was angry. It made that grunting, growling sound again, then turned its back on us and walked away into the trees.

We got out of there right away as we were both afraid the thing might change its mind and come back towards us. The whole incident was probably less than a minute. We didn't go walking in that area anymore after seeing it, I know it was a Bigfoot."

In a follow up interview, the man told me he was convinced he and his friend had seen a Bigfoot. He also believes the creature was angry at their presence and that had they stayed, or returned, the creature would have become more aggressive.

David Weatherly exploring Sitgreaves National Forest (photo by author)

Apache Country & Native Encounters

On the White Mountain Apache lands, in eastern Arizona, tribal members have long spoken of the existence of the "hairy man." There's a long history of Sasquatch sightings and encounters in the region. Much of the land is undeveloped and includes high elevation forests. The reservation also runs into the Apache-Sitgreaves National Forest, creating a vast area of prime habitat for animals, and, according to native legends, Bigfoot.

The Fort Apache Reservation is home to the White Mountain Apache Tribe. The reservation is 2,627 square miles and home to over twelve thousand people. For centuries, the Apaches have been aware of the existence of the hairy creatures living in the forest. By nature, tribal members are quiet about such matters, but in the early 2000s, many decided to break their silence and speak out about the growing number of encounters occurring on tribal land.

For a time, there was even a display of footprint casts at the White Mountain Apache Tribal police headquarters in Whiteriver. This is due, in part, to Whiteriver being a hotspot of bigfoot sightings. It's also the largest community on the reservation.

There are many accounts in Apache country, reports of large, hairy creatures running across back roads and highways, raiding farms and gardens, and of course, being sighted near water sources.

More incidents are surfacing all the time. As tribal spokeswoman Collette Altaha notes:

"We're not prone to easily talk to outsiders, but there have been more sightings than ever before. It cannot be ignored any longer."

Scott Davis, reporter for Tucson's Channel 3, was among those who covered the story of the tribe's new attitude of openness about Bigfoot. He spoke to numerous members of the White Mountain nation. As he reported:

"Footprints in the mud. Tufts of hair on a fence. Ear-piercing screeches in the night. These are only fragments of the stories now coming from the White Mountains in Eastern Arizona.

"No one's had a negative encounter with it," said Marjorie Grimes, who lives in Whitewater, the primary town on the reservation. Grimes is one of many who claim to have seen the creature over the last 25 years. Her first sighting was in 1982. Her most recent was in the summer of 2004, driving home from the town of Cibecue. She becomes more animated as the memory comes forth.

"It was all black and it was tall! The way it walked; it was taking big strides. I put on the brakes and raced back and looked between the two trees where it was, and it was gone!

Grimes' son, Francis, has a story. Their neighbor Cecil Hendricks has a story. Even police officers have had strange encounters. Officer Katherine Montoya has seen it twice. On a recent Monday night, dozens of people called into the tribe's radio station, KNNB, to talk about what they'd seen. Others came in person."

Although it was a big decision for the tribe to finally speak out about encounters with the creatures, many people on the reservation supported the idea. After so many years, and so many accounts, tribal members felt it was the right time and that the widespread interest in Bigfoot would make it easier for outsiders to listen and not discount their reports. As Davis' report stated, every step met with both resistance and acceptance:

"...the decision to let 3TV report this story was a controversial

one. On the radio program, one Apache caller said tribal elders were uncomfortable letting the legend be known. Still, Altaha believes it is the right thing to do.

"I've heard stories from a while back about sightings. I'm not easily persuaded, but with so many of the people coming forward and telling us their stories...there might be something out there that actually exists."

Tribal police lieutenant, Ray Burnett, puts it in terms of public safety:

"A couple of times, they've seen this creature looking through windows. They're scared when they call."

Members of the tribal police have even made plaster casts of prints found during investigations of sightings, and tufts of hair and other materials have been gathered at the scenes of some encounters. The department sent their samples to the State Department of Public Safety for analysis in their crime lab.

As least one sample was determined to be animal hair of "unknown species or origin." Further testing was reportedly taking place, but no follow up statement has been released. Unfortunately, no major State or Federal agency formally investigates Bigfoot sightings, so there are few resources to use in such cases.

But people on the Apache reservation do take the accounts seriously, and so do members of the tribal police.

As Davis' noted in closing his story:

"...on the reservation, Lieutenant Burnette wants outsiders to realize that the department takes these calls seriously, and so should you.

"The calls we're getting from people—they weren't hallucinating, they weren't drunks, they weren't people that we know can make hoax calls. They're from real citizens of the Fort Apache Indian Reservation."

Hawley Lake, a site sitting at an elevation of 8,200 feet, sees heavy recreational use during the summer months, it is often inaccessible for much of the winter due to heavy snowfall. There have been several reported encounters from the lake over the years.

During some of my own investigations in the state, one man told me about an encounter he and his brother had in 2010 while camping at the lake:

"It was late fall of 2010 and starting to get really cold up on the mountain. My brother and I were up at Hawley lake camping. It was the middle of the week and there wasn't anyone else around, at least not where we were. The first night, it was pretty quiet. The second night, things got a little creepy. I woke up and had to use the bathroom. I got out of the tent, went beyond our camp area, and stood by some trees to relieve myself. I was almost finished when I heard something hit the ground near me. I thought it was probably a branch falling and ignored it. But then it happened again. Then a third time. The third time, whatever hit bounced a little and I knew that stuff was being thrown. I thought it was my brother screwing around so I shouted at him. I was pretty tired and pissed so I shouted some profanities. When I did, more stuff was thrown, and whatever was tossed, it sounded bigger. Then there was a loud crash near me and I saw that it was a big piece of a tree, like a piece of the trunk. It looked heavy and I thought, my brother probably couldn't throw that very far. I hurried back to the tent and when I climbed in, I realized my brother was inside and was fast asleep. This really freaked me out! I didn't really sleep anymore that night and when the sun came up, I got up too.

I went over to the area where I'd had the experience. All over the place, there were pieces from a tree. Some were pretty big and didn't look like something a man could throw easy. I told my brother what had happened, and he said that early in the night, he thought someone was walking around in our camp. He figured it was some other campers or something maybe trying to steal some beer or whatever, not that we had any.

But the big thing was later that afternoon. We were down by the lake, sitting on some rocks drinking some coffee we had made. My brother got a funny look and said, "What's that?"

He was pointing across to another part of the lake's bank. Someone, or something was squatting down dipping their hands into the water. We both stared at it. The hair on my arms went up and I said, "that's not a man."

It's like the thing knew we were staring at it. It suddenly looked right at us, then it stood up. It had to have been about seven or eight feet tall. It stood straight up, and I felt like it was pissed we were looking at it. It turned and walked away.

We packed up and left right away and never went back up there. I am sure that we saw a bigfoot."

The White Mountain Independent reported on Bigfoot in their March 26, 2010 edition. According to the article, an impressive set of tracks was found on the banks of the White River earlier that month. Former law enforcement officer and Bigfoot researcher, A.K. Riley was on the scene to take measurements and photos.

According to the story by reporter Mike Leiby:

"A.K. Riley, former lawman in the community and renowned Bigfoot investigator, found a cache of new prints in the hills surrounding the area, saying he discovered them about middle of last week.

Riley gave the Independent exclusive access to the prints, which came out of the dense, brush-covered hills overlooking Whiteriver onto an extremely rough dirt trail/road, leaving around 20 feet of them before crossing over to the other side and continuing for about another 30 feet or so and then disappearing into the woods.

Riley said he was in the area performing his normal searches for signs of Bigfoot when he came upon the fresh prints, indicating the creature may be on the move again with the snow melting and it being easier to move about in the rough terrain.

Riley pointed out other tracks in the area that were clearly made by humans, noting the size difference in the tracks and lamenting the fact that the site's integrity had been compromised by the presence of those curious about the prints and the area's legend of the creature.

"You can see where they have put their feet beside them to show how much bigger they are, but it messes up the prints and makes them hard to see sometimes."

Riley took the reporter to another location on the banks of the White River where another set of tracks had been previously found. While some of the track was washed away, there was still the clear impression of a large, deep heel, and the faded trace of toes that had dug into the soil. The print was about 13 inches long and about four or five inches wide.

"These have been here for some time," said Riley, pointing at the faded earlier print by the river bank. "And you can see some others in the area as well, but they are faint and hard to see, but they were left here by Bigfoot too, probably a few days ago, but with the snow melting you cannot see them very well now."

On the Trail in Arizona (photo by author)

The researcher told Leiby the creature was likely looking for food, or simply traveling along using the river as a guide to its destination. Riley is confident in the existence of the creature, as the *Independent* story noted:

"A woman who lives in Whiteriver and passes on information to and from Riley in his research said she too believes in the existence of the creature. She said on at least two occasions she has seen evidence and heard noises compelling her to believe something is out there.

The woman asked to remain anonymous but said she and her daughter were out in their truck one evening and saw "something" cross the road in front of them that was "big and hairy" with about a three-to-four-foot stride, which was able to cross the double-lane road in no more than three steps. She said on another occasion a friend of hers witnessed what she believed was Bigfoot in an abandoned trailer. The woman apparently heard some noise in a single-wide trailer and when she went in to investigate saw what she thinks was Bigfoot hunched over on a corner of the trailer trying to hide."

According to the report, there are those in the region who try to dismiss the accounts and even track finds, preferring perhaps to believe the creature is only a myth. But the accounts have been talked about for years. Loggers and others who work in the woods, rangers, outdoorsmen, and even police officers.

Riley spoke further about Bigfoot in a follow up story done by NBC news on April 7th:

"You can feel it. It's like someone's watching you," Riley said, standing on a dirt road in the middle of the woods on the White Mountain Apache Indian Reservation.

Within the last two weeks, Riley found a trail of "Bigfoot" prints on that very road, which he says are proof. His search for the elusive creature began four years ago when he says local pets started missing, some turning up mutilated, and sightings of a Bigfoot were made in the area."

"They needed a Bigfoot investigator," Riley explained, "so I kind of went along with it, and as I neared retirement, I figured I'd make it my hobby."

Riley became much more serious about his 'hobby' after he saw one of the creatures himself. Describing it, he stated:

"It was tall, and we just sat there, and we froze. It was frightening."

Riley rummages through a room in his home and minutes later, comes out to show us that his four-year search has turned up more than just footprints—he has collected hair, pictures of shelters made of tree branches, and even a very fuzzy black and white photograph taken by a trip camera at 5 A.M. one morning last May.

He explains that from the various sizes of footprints he's found over the course of his investigation, he believes there's not one Bigfoot, but a family of four living in the area year round."

Riley gets a lot of leads and witnesses from officials at the local Game and Fish Department. While they don't formally investigate such calls themselves, they have no qualms about passing the sightings along to Riley, and at least one official even helps out on occasion unofficially.

Manuelita Kanty, who works for the Game and Fish department often looks into accounts if Riley is not available, passing any information along to the investigator. Kanty believes Riley is on the trail of a genuine creature:

"I don't think he's crazy, because I've heard my grandfather talk of it."

A notable and impressive track find was made in the summer of 2013.

The case started when numerous people reported strange animal vocalizations in the small town of Tsaile, Apache county, in the northeastern portion of the state. The town is on the Navajo Nation and many locals have great familiarity with area wildlife. The sounds could not be identified and occurred several nights running.

One morning, after hearing the strange sounds, locals discovered a long trackway of large, barefoot prints. The visibility of the trackway was due to a heavy rain the previous night, making the ground muddy. Prime material for capturing evidence and sign of wildlife.

Johnny and Carol Willeto documented the track find and well-known Bigfoot researcher, Cliff Barackman conducted a further investigation. Prints were documented at 13 inches in length, 6.5 inches in width at the ball of the foot and 4 inches in width at the heel. Step length was calculated to be 61 inches.

The tracks came from Canyon del Muerto and ran to the edge of Tsaile Lake. The prints went into the lake, and then, back out. Fish carcasses and half eaten fish were found littering the shore around the lake where the prints were discovered.

The trackway continued north through the desert along a shallow ditch that paralleled the road a hundred yards to its east. The trail was lost when it turned to a gravel road towards a forested mountain area.

In the report on his Website, Barackman stated he found the trackway interesting for several reasons, noting it revealed aspects of the creature's behavior:

"The trackway reveals some interesting behaviors of the sasquatch that made it. It emerged from the roadless area of Canyon del Muerto and led to Tsaile Lake where it entered the lake to catch a fish. One can speculate that this might have been a regular stop on its rounds, especially if fishing with one's hands could score a fat meal with ease. It discarded the leftover fish on the shore before heading north. The path it took was not on the easily-traveled dirt road, but rather in a shallow ditch about one hundred yards to the east of that road."

Barackman stated the creature would have been exposed during this portion of its journey and the ditch would be the only cover offered. As to the case in general, he believes it to be an especially interesting one that leaves little room for speculation.

"Many people in the community saw the footprints, and there was very little doubt as to what left them. When one combines the previous night's frightening vocalizations (a common occurrence that summer), the size of the footprints, the distance between them, the dead fish on the lake shore, and the fact that the track maker was barefoot for over two miles of difficult, prickly, pokey walking, the only conclusion that can be arrived at is that a sasquatch made the prints. For the Navajos seeing these prints, there was no doubt. Soon after the discovery of the footprints, several people in the community observed sasquatches nearby, and their sounds continued to be heard periodically throughout the rest of the season."

A report from Apache County, recorded on the GCBRO (Gulf Coast Bigfoot Research Organization) Website involved a strange creature crossing the road in front of a couple on a clear day.

It was July 2, 1979 when the couple enjoyed a picnic lunch at a location called "Sheep's Crossing." After finishing their meal, the pair packed up and headed off for a drive to Greer, AZ to visit a friend. According to the witness, it was a sunny, cloudless day and they were riding with the top down on the car:

"I remember as if it were yesterday, driving down an unobscured section of straight, paved, road (with pine forest on either side), when a figure began to cross the road beginning from approximately 100 yds. in front of us, from right to left. It was slightly slouched with its back to us and appeared to be no taller than five feet six inches, completely covered in reddish brown fur and using its knuckles to traverse the road (as an ape might walk)."

Understandably, the witnesses were both shocked at seeing the odd creature and pulled the car over immediately. The creature had entered the forest and was out of sight. No further movement was noticed in the trees.

The witness got out of his car and looked for tracks along the creature's route, but nothing was discovered. The witness then drove around the area a bit more, hoping to have another sighting, but nothing else occurred. He didn't report his encounter until 2011, owing to skeptical responses received from the people he talked to after the incident.

"...what I saw was the full back-side of a creature (it didn't turn its face toward us), that walked erect (slightly hunched over and with limited assistance of knuckles from its long arms) that was no taller than 5'6 and covered in reddish-brown fur. The sighting occurred, starting from approximately 100 yds away and continued to approximately 50 yds proximity, while lasting only about 15 seconds."

Northeast of the Fort Apache Reservation, and still within the White Mountains, lies the town of Springerville. Springerville is a community of about two thousand people and has a variety of terrain including mountains, prairies and wooded areas.

The GCBRO received an interesting account about an incident that occurred in the area in 1998. The sighting was around eleven o'clock at night in late September, but the reporting witness couldn't recall the exact day of the month.

The account involves the reporting witnesses' brother and sister in law, who were staying with her parents. The residence was a mobile home in a populated area. The back of the property is a wooded area that turns into prairie after a few hundred yards, and eventually runs into the White Mountains.

A family dog was outside and making so much noise that people in the home couldn't get to sleep. The man went out to try to quiet the animal and determine why it was so excited.

"My brother states that he went out and saw that the dog was barking toward the line of woods in back of the mobile home. My brother stated that he scanned the tree line and noticed that there was something big just out of sight and mostly hidden by trees.

He stated that he noticed there were two huge "red" eyes looking back at him and the barking dog. My brother, feeling brave, started to walk toward whatever it was but states that after a few steps, he got the feeling inside that it was not safe to go out any further. At that point, he sent the dog out to get whatever it was and after running a few yards, the dog also stopped in its tracks and did not go any further. "

The man returned to the house, intending to get another

family member to go back outside with him. However, once inside, he discovered everyone else had fallen asleep while he had been investigating.

He went back out again and found that, although the dog was still barking, whatever had been at the back of the property was gone. The man again returned to the house and went to bed. As to the details of the creature, according to the report:

"My brother states that what he saw was not a bear but was covered in hair and appeared to walk on two legs."

The report further states ranchers and other residents in the area had reported incidents of pets and farm animals being killed.

Hairy Men in the Desert

While sightings in the deep southern portion of Arizona are far fewer, there are still some accounts of interest. The land is much drier in the south, and although there are still national forests and mountains, there are also stretches of flat land. If large, undiscovered creatures lived in the region, they would have to be intelligent enough to find water and remain hidden.

Graham County in the state's southeast section lies northeast of Tucson. Much of its terrain is desert, but it also holds the Pinaleno Mountains. The Pinaleno Mountains are one of Arizona's "sky islands." The sky islands are isolated mountain ranges separated by broad, high desert valleys. Mt. Graham, sitting at an elevation of 10,720 feet, is the highest point in the Pinalenos. The region has been the location of several interesting accounts. Numerous people camping or hiking in the mountains have heard strange animal-like "whooping" sounds, wood knocks, and rock clacking, all of which are noted as being connected to Bigfoot sightings.

One witness reported on an incident from the winter of 2007. It was January 22nd when the witness was traveling to work through snow and fog. Moving at about fifteen miles per hour through the foothills of Mt. Graham, the witness saw a large, bipedal creature run across the road.

The man reported the creature was at least seven feet tall and hairy. The man described the creature's motion as a "slow run" and said it seemed startled when the car's headlights illuminated it. Its hair was dark brown and looked matted. No further details were noted due to the heavy fog.

A fascinating encounter from 1977 was reported to the BFRO by a military man. The sighting took place near Benson, a small town off Interstate 10, southeast of Tucson.

It was sometime in July 1977 when the soldier boarded a military bus at Fort Huachuca and headed north. The bus hit Highway 10 and around ten to fifteen minutes north of Benson, the driver pulled over. The man reports that he was the only person who remained on the bus. Sitting on the driver's side of the vehicle, he looked out at the surrounding area. Conditions were clear and sunny, and he states he could "see for miles."

On the far side of the road was a white house, possibly a ranch. An 18-wheeler was coming down the far side of the road headed south. Just as the big rig passed, the witness saw something come up out of a gully on the far side of the road. He described the sight:

"My first thought was, is that a bear? Then as the thing kept coming up the embankment, I could see that it was walking on two feet, that's when my mind then asked, is that a Gorilla? I remember it was dark tan in color, with long hair, you could also see it was very muscular, and it had these long, flowing arms. As it came up the embankment, it turned its head, and it was like time stopped. When I looked in its face, I actually saw man like features. It's hard to explain, but it was like a big, hairy man. From its facial expression, I could tell it was frightened. It actually ran with its head looking back for a good distance."

In follow up interviews with BFRO investigators, the witness, John, stated he was sure the creature was frightened by the 18-wheeler. He also noted he could see the creature's chest when it turned to look back at the highway. The bigfoot turned away from the highway and ran along a road that led to the white ranch John had seen. The sighting left him stunned.

"I sat there, for oh, at least 45 seconds, watching it run up this road. You should have seen how fast it could run, and how long the strides were, it was amazing. It was also very hot that day, as days are in Arizona, but it was like it ran with ease. Then it turned off the road to the left, and it was gone, into the desert. I just sat there in disbelief for a long time, and then realized what I just witnessed, a sighting of Bigfoot itself."

Another military man, a retired veteran, shared his account on the BFRO Website. It details an encounter he had between Sierra Vista and Tombstone in Cochise County.

According to the witness, the event occurred in 1972 when, as a young man, he was hunting with his father and a man named Chuck, a friend of his father's. It was winter when the trio were out along the banks of the San Pedro River off Charlestone Road. As the witness recalls:

"As we were walking along the river (not really a river but more a large creek), we all came to a sudden stop when we heard this "animal or thing" scream so loud that it made me freeze. I looked at my father to see that he had turned ash white along with his friend Chuck. My father quickly changed out his shotgun shell for a magnum load. We beat a hasty retreat out of there and called it a day."

The man recalls the scream lasting five to seven seconds and that it rose from a low pitch to a high one. Neither Chuck or the witnesses' father, both experienced hunters, had ever heard a sound like it before. Of note is the fact that Chuck had observed something else unusual:

"At the time I did not know that my father's friend Chuck, had seen movement in some mesquite trees about 30 yards away from the direction the sound was coming from. As we departed the area, Chuck saw large footprints in the sand of the San Pedro River, I am not sure how we did not see them before."

Interestingly, the encounter took place in what is now the San Pedro Riparian Conservation Area. Managed by the BLM (Bureau of Land Management), the area is considered a sensitive ecosystem with year round water flow and an abundance of wildlife, including Mule deer, javelina and a wide range of birds.

Further south, the Huachuca Mountains in Cochise County were the site of another encounter with a sasquatch. According to the Bigfoot Encounters Website (bigfootencounters.com), three friends were on a hiking/camping trip in the Huachuca Mountains when the incident occurred.

The reporting witness, Jeff Smith of Arizona, writes that the encounter took place in 2011. Heavy wildfires that year had restricted available trails, and the group ended up near Miller Canyon where they went off path and camped.

All three were in a domed tent, about 20 yards off a dirt road. Smith says he was awoken in the middle of the night to find his friend sitting up in his sleeping bag yelling. Once the man calmed, he told Smith he had seen a Bigfoot looking through the top of the tent where there was only mesh. Smith was a bit doubtful but noted the grave look on his friend's face. Two years later, he again spoke to the man about the incident. His friend was adamant about what he'd seen:

"Dude, I saw it. I know what I saw and still remember it. I wasn't dreaming. It's just as vivid as when it happened. I looked up through the tent and saw its face looking at me. The moon was bright and behind where it was standing, making it hard to distinguish facial features. I could see a perfect silhouette. Its head was pretty long, and it didn't really have a neck. Its head seemed to just merge with its shoulders. It was big—at least 8 ft. It was standing over the tent, like it was leaning forward and looking through the moon roof netting. I could see what looked like whites of its eyes. We stared at each other for at least 30 seconds before it was gone."

Conclusion

The sightings recounted here represent only a small portion of the encounters that have taken place in the Grand Canyon state. Tourists continue to flock to the state every year to enjoy skiing, hiking, camping and other outdoor activities.

With its vast wilderness areas, numerous mountain ranges and resources, it's likely we'll continue to hear more and more about strange creature encounters in Arizona.

The newer, open attitude taken by Native Americans has the potential to bring forth a wealth of knowledge about the unknown creatures dwelling in the sparsely populated areas of the state, as well.

With sweeping vistas, one of the world's seven natural wonders, amazing sunsets...and monsters, there's plenty of fascinating things to find in Arizona.

The Company They Keep

by Timothy Renner

In 1886 there were no streetlights between the Mt. Nebo Church, just outside of Delta, Pennsylvania and what is now Cooper Road. There were no homes or garages along the way with floodlights or dusk-to-dawn LED illuminations. There may have been a few homes with candles in the window or gas lamps glowing dimly from a room where someone read or did their evening work. All this is to note that the mile or so between the place where Mt. Nebo Church sat on Slate Hill and Cooper Road would have been quite dark and equally lonesome in the fall of 1886.

Nehemiah "Nemiah" Cooper, his wife Mary, and some unnamed friends were making their way home from evening services at Mt. Nebo Church in the Autumn of 1886 when they saw something on the ground which caught their attention. It seemed small at first - about the size of a bucket - but sprang up from the ground, revealing its massive size. They described it as a "strange monster" 12 or 15 feet tall and 6 or 7 feet across the shoulders. Being that it was late October, they first assumed the creature to be a prank - perhaps a Halloween trick of some sort - so they began to pelt the monster with stones. When the creature began to advance on the party, they realized it was no trick, and discretion being the better part of valor, they decided the safety of a home was a better place to spend the night than a dark and lonely road.

The whole area in this small section of southeastern York County was thought to be haunted - from the Muddy Creek bridge on Paper

Mill Road, over Slate Hill to the Mason/Dixon line in the south, and to Peach Bottom and the Susquehanna River eastward. Few people were brave enough to travel these roads at night in the 1800s. Besides a headless ghost known to stalk these grounds, there were unnamed things not only said to be frightful, but also *dangerous*. The African-American cemetery was said to be an area of which the nighttime traveler should be especially wary. The headless ghost above was presumably the spirit of the man whose headless body was rumored to have been found in one of the nearby slate quarries - not the only human corpse that was said to have been found in the area slate mines.

The McConkey Mansion, built sometime in the late 1700s, was located in this region as well. It too was said to have been haunted. A strange mist was known to hang around the mansion. Weird colored will-o-the-wisps were seen around the grounds, sometimes gliding down the walls of the house before making their way out to the river. Rhododendron and ferns grew wildly about the old place, except in two "fairy rings" - round patches, greener than the surrounding growth, encircled by tall grass. Horses would stop at a certain point near the mansion, and refuse to proceed. Because the McConkey family came from Ireland, some said a leprechaun made its home on the grounds. The tall shadowy figures seen in the woods around the mansion would suggest something else was also making its home here.

A little bit west of The McConkey Mansion, in the 1920s, Sam Glidden and his sister Ammie were holding regular seances at their Slateville home. Ammie would go into trances, eyes shut, furiously writing the words of the spirits as dictated from beyond while Sam fed her paper after paper. The spirits told them many things, including tales of pirates sailing up the Susquehanna River and landing at Peach Bottom. Their buried gold was never found, but Ammie wrote on in her ghostly script.

The Mason/Dixon trail cuts through a beautiful, thickly wooded section right beside Muddy Creek, all the way to the Susquehanna River. Hemlock, mountain laurel, and rhododendron grow through the riparian gorge. It was here, in 1972, that ecology teacher Bob Chance and some students got their canoe stuck in the creek. They came to retrieve the boat a few days later and on the hike out were pelted by stones thrown by something unseen on the hills above. Bob went on to investigate many bigfoot sightings in the area, including several I will talk about in this article.

In the 1970s bigfoot became a household name as popular shows such as *In Search Of...* featured stories on the creatures. Perhaps after bigfoot entered pop culture the creatures became easier to discuss - or perhaps people finally had a name to put to what they were seeing. For these reasons, or for whatever reason, sightings began to pick up in the 1970s.

The BFRO records a report of sightings of a "hairy man-like creature" near Muddy Creek from the years 1973-1976. Seen multiple times by campers, students, and hunters this creature was said to be covered in hair, nearly seven feet tall, and with a gait measuring nearly four feet. The creature, or creatures, were thought to be living in or around the slate quarries which pepper the region. Most of these quarries were long abandoned by the 1970s.

In a wooded area off of Atom Road, in the summer of 1974, a family had set up a temporary home in a camper while their new house was being finished. The parents had taken jobs at the then-new Peach Bottom Atomic Power Station. Their three children, a girl, aged 3, and two boys, 7 and 9, were playing happily in the woods when they heard a snapping twig. Looking in the direction of the sound, they noticed first long fingers - too long to be those of a human, with dark skin visible through a thin growth of hair. The hands were grasping a tree, behind which stood the creature. It had approached through the brush without making a sound and stood just 10 feet away, watching the children.

Looking upward they saw a face that could have been human, but for the growth of brown hair on the 6½ foot tall creature. Caked with mud, matted and unkempt, the hair grew closely around the eyes. This, in combination with the large hands, convinced the two older children they were not looking at a human being, but something else entirely. They started to run. The 7-year-old called to his older brother to retrieve their sister. Bravely, he turned, gathered up his youngest sibling and the three children made their way quickly to the camper.

The family left immediately and never stayed another night in that camper. They had heard of other bigfoot sightings in the area and decided not to take any chances. A few weeks later the father went to retrieve the camper and found it missing. A quick search located the camper down the hill from where they abandoned it, floating at the edge of the Susquehanna River. No humans had permission or reason to be on the remote, private land. It was suspected that the bigfoot creature had pushed the camper down the hill.

Just west of Mt. Nebo church in 1975, another family claimed a bigfoot creature was coming onto their property with some regularity. At night, they would hear its howling screams far off - which would turn into a low grunt as the creature approached their house. Sometimes the creature was loud enough to wake the family from their sleep. Area dogs would bark and howl, disturbed by the creature's presence. On occasion the creature would pick up and move their garbage cans and at least one time they heard it come up onto the back porch of their home. In the family's words, the creature was "haunting" them.

1978 was a very strange year in York County. UFO reports came in frequently - including an especially strange case of a craft landing, not too far at all from Delta, in the blink-and-you'll-miss-it town of Gatchellville. There were other reports of strange lights seen above Peach Bottom Atomic Power Station. 1978 also brought more sightings of large, bipedal, hair-covered creatures throughout the county - quite a few of them around the Delta / Peach Bottom area.

The Hilsmeier farm sits above Muddy Creek - just over the hill from the place where Bob Chance and his students were pelted by stones from an unknown assailant. On the night of January 27, 1978, something greatly upset the Hilsmeier family dogs. The two German shepherds were barking loudly and running from their house out to the fields and back again, repeatedly - as if to say "something is out here." It was unusual for the dogs to be so aggravated.

The following morning, Allen Hilsmeier and his sons found weird three-toed footprints criss-crossing their land. The tracks were each sixteen inches in length and six inches in width. The depth of each footprint seemed to indicate that it was left by something with a considerable weight. The stride of the creature was measured at about five feet. This stride did not vary - even when going up steep hills. Each footprint fell in line with the previous - they were not offset like human tracks.

Some two thousand tracks were left in the icy snow around the Hilsmeier farm - across two miles of rugged terrain, over barbed wire fences, through the woods, across a creek, and over a distant hill. The trackway terminated strangely, in the middle of a field, with no indication of where the creature went from that point. Long, coarse hair was found stuck to the barbed wire. Along the trackway were found the remains of a rabbit: blood, hair, and a leg - presumed to have been eaten by the creature - and a dead calf. The calf was confirmed to have died of natural causes by its owner, but something had been eating at the corpse.

On the night of February 26, 1978, Jeffry Meriman and Daniel Givler, two security guards at Peach Bottom Atomic Power Station, heard eerie shrieks in the woods around the plant visitors center. A later investigation would find huge bare footprints around the center. More footprints would be found along Paper Mill Road, near the Power Station, on March 1.

It was 11:00 pm on March 2, 1978, when Norval Thomas, a truck driver from Baltimore, MD, made his way to Peach Bottom Atomic Power Station with a delivery of fuel oil. The haunted McConkey Mansion would have sat on the hill above him, just a few years before, but now the mansion itself was just a ghost, torn down to make way for the Power Station. In the beams of the truck's headlights Thomas saw a dark form cross the road.

As he passed the figure, Thomas realized it was in the shape of a man, over seven feet tall. "I never saw a man that big in my life," Thomas said to himself, before realizing that no humans should be in the area at night - restricted as it was, and with thick woods on either side of the road.

Thomas pulled into the station and told the security guards what he had seen. Urlo C. Williams, sergeant of plant security, along with Thomas and some other employees from the Power Station grabbed some flashlights and went back up the road to the location of Thomas' sighting.

They found huge footprints - almost twice the length of a man's size 10½ boot, with a stride measuring 4 to 5 feet between tracks - and they heard loud, shrill, chilling squeals. "Like a pig's squeal, but it wasn't a pig," said Williams. "It made your skin crawl." Donald Johnson, who lived about a mile from the Power Station, reported that his dogs were "going berserk" at about midnight on the same evening.

Back on the Hilsmeier farm, in the summer of 1978, with the windows open to catch the cool night breeze, Margaret Hilsmeier, wife of Allen, was up late, the last one awake in the house. She heard a series of frightening, roaring howls coming from the direction of Muddy Creek. She described the howls as sounding like "Mighty Joe Young", the giant gorilla of movie fame, and said whatever creature issued the sounds must have had immense lung capacity - for the howls were not only loud in volume but of great duration as well.

In 2011 a woman living in a cabin off of Orchard Road, less than a mile east of Cooper Road, was on her back patio when something caused her to look into the trees behind her home. She saw at her fence line, about 25 feet from her, the black silhouette of a huge, upright thing, its red eyes glowing some 8 feet off the ground. She noticed a peculiar bad smell around her home that evening.

Another haunted house, known locally as the "Suicide House" was located on Grove Road, due east of the Hilsmeier Farm. The Suicide House was so named for a local legend which stated a woman killed herself on the upper floor of the dwelling. Local children, it was said, never walked past the property - they would always run past the Suicide House. A couple living there during the years of 2013-2015 reported shadowy figures around the grounds, as well as unexplained sounds from the surrounding woods. Once, the couple was in the woods on their property when they heard a loud howl which frightened them enough to send them running back to the relative safety of their haunted home. The Suicide House, like McConkey Mansion, has been torn down. A new home now stands on the property.

The above sightings span over 130 years, but they are all located in the same area. Not only are they located in the same state, county, and township - but they are all in an area of roughly 8 square miles. These are only the sightings that I have found thus far. I am convinced that I will find more over time, and that there are many more that I will never hear about - due to the reluctance of witnesses to come forward with stories of the unusual - or because witnesses have died or moved away before I could hear their stories.

A cluster of bigfoot sightings and other strangeness in just 8 square miles, down in the southeastern corner of York County, Pennsylvania. It bears repeating: 8 square miles! There have been other bigfoot sightings not far away as well - in 1978 a man in the nearby town of Fawn Grove witnessed a 10 foot tall hair covered biped with glowing white eyes and a pungent stench. North of Delta in the same year, a hunter saw a creature running through the woods along the river near Holtwood Dam. In 2015, just north of the Holtwood Dam beside the Indian Steps Museum in Airville, another witness reported an awful stench, like dead flesh mixed with skunk, and heard something very large which stayed just out of sight but paced him through the woods. I have been drawn to this tight cluster of sightings in the Delta / Peach Bottom area with all of the attendant questions. Why is this happening here? How can this be?

If bigfoot creatures are natural animals, like bears, mountain lions, or even gorillas, then there can only be two answers as I see things. Either there is a breeding population of bigfoot in Delta, Pennsylvania which has stayed in the area for over a century, or the creatures move through the area with great frequency and regularity.

If you look at the area on Google Satellite you will, hopefully, see the problem with the idea of a breeding population of giant ape-men around Delta, Pennsylvania. There are beautiful, dense patches of woodland and fertile river bottoms with multiple creeks winding their way to the Susquehanna in this section. It is perhaps my favorite hiking in the county, and well worth the effort if you ever get to this area. However, is there really enough wild land to hide a breeding population of bigfoot - be it clans or family groups or however these creatures organize themselves for mating? Is there really enough remote woodland to hide young bigfoot who are bound to be less experienced than the adults and therefore more likely to make mistakes and be seen - and possibly even to be shot, given the amount of hunters and open-carry gun owners in York County? I suppose it's possible, but it seems extremely unlikely.

The daily caloric requirements for a natural animal the size of a bigfoot creature would have to be extreme. There is plenty of wildlife in the area, as well as local livestock. More than a few of these farms have reported livestock deaths under mysterious circumstances. One farm, just outside of my "area of interest" in this article was the scene of a bloody massacre when something opened a chicken coop door and killed all 30 of the feathered occupants. The heads of the birds looked to have been twisted off, the breasts ripped open, and the blood sucked from the animals. Huge three-toed footprints led to and from the gory scene. Local dogs, too, have been found dead under mysterious circumstances - sometimes torn to pieces and sometimes thrown or otherwise placed high in trees. Sometimes both. I have also taken reports of mysterious deer kills and of deer legs found hanging in trees, bent at the crook - gruesomely balanced upon a branch.

There are, of course, for an omnivore as bigfoot is reported to be, vegetarian options as well. There are large orchards of apple and peach trees - at least one located directly in the Delta / Peach Bottom area covered in this article - not to mention our native fruit trees, the oft-forgotten pawpaw which still grow wild throughout the wooded sections along the Susquehanna River. There are berries - both wild and domestic growing throughout the region. There are commercial and residential gardens - vast fields of corn, soy, and common garden vegetables.

I have often read that if an area can support bears or other large predators, it can support bigfoot. There have been reports of a large black bear in the Muddy Creek region, and there is bear sign on some trees along the creek. Though the Pennsylvania Game Commission will never admit to their presence (like bigfoot!), if you talk to enough outdoorsmen in the area, you will hear stories of mountain lions. I believe these stories as I saw a cougar myself, just south of the Mason/ Dixon line in Maryland, on two consecutive days.

So, yes, there seems to be an abundance of food options as well as other large omnivores, like bears, and top-of-the-food-chain predators, like cougars, in the area in question. Let's stop and think about that for a moment though, in terms of bigfoot. This means that this relatively small area would now have to be host to not only a breeding population of bigfoot, but bears and likely cougars as well! Not only would the area have to host the creatures, but it would have to *hide* them - for none of these things - bear, cougar, or bigfoot - are commonplace sights; and all of them seem to want to stay out of the way of humans, for the most part. Once again, I have to say the idea of a native breeding population of bigfoot creatures in the Delta / Peach Bottom area, considering the factors above, just seems incredibly unlikely.

The second option, if these creatures are natural animals, provides a far more likely explanation: The bigfoot creatures move through the area with some regularity. This option carries it's own set of questions: How do they travel into and out of the area without being seen more often than they are? Why do they travel through this area? How often are they here? From where are they going and do they have a regular destination which brings them through south-central Pennsylvania in general, and this small section of York County in particular? If it is a migratory pattern, it is not based on the seasons - for the creatures have been reported at all times of the year, for over 130 years. (Nemiah Cooper's encounter was just the earliest I could find, by the way - I am certain there are earlier encounters from the area, either lost to time or as yet uncovered by your author.)

This leads to what tends to be a very uncomfortable question for many bigfoot enthusiasts - but it is a question which nevertheless must be asked. What if these creatures are not natural animals as we know them? There is a certain segment of readers now rolling their eyes and hissing "woo, woo" (that derisive slang in the bigfoot community for anything supposedly supernatural or paranormal attributed to the creatures). I understand. I really do. You want to be taken seriously and accepted science already scoffs at the idea of bigfoot. If we start adding other strangeness into the equation we're never going to be taken seriously.

I doubt we will ever be taken seriously by the mainstream anyway. My book, *Bigfoot in Pennsylvania,* is a collection of newspaper articles describing what I believe to be bigfoot encounters in Pennsylvania dating back to the 1830s. Besides the description of many, many bigfoot behaviors still noted by witnesses today, there is another common factor found throughout the articles: the ridicule and derision of bigfoot witnesses by skeptics. Witnesses are often accused of being drunk, crazy, stupid, or of mistaking bears, other people, and even raccoons for giant, hairy wild-men. This drum has been beaten for a long, long time.

Let us ask ourselves some questions: What if a bigfoot creature is never found - alive or dead? What if, after all of our seeking, we are still only left with some footprints, hair, and scat of unknown origin? The Patterson-Gimlin film is an incredible piece of footage and I am convinced it shows a real creature - but many others are not convinced, and no matter how many experts testify on the proportion of the creature shown in the film, the inhuman gait, the flexing muscles showing beneath the hair, or the absolute inability of costume makers at the time to craft such a convincing suit, there will always be a huge segment of the population, both expert and layman, who insist the footage is faked. This film is arguably the most convincing piece of evidence we have for the existence of bigfoot and it is regularly dismissed out of hand.

It seems that every bit of evidence we gather is derided and declared inconclusive at best, bogus at worst. At some point, we must ask ourselves why. Why do game cameras never seem to snap a convincing image of these creatures, though other elusive animals have been captured with some regularity (cougars, for instance)? Why do cell phone batteries and other electronic devices so often fail in the presence of these creatures? Why do the best images and film footage, taken by researchers who have devoted their life to finding these creatures, so often come down to blurry "blobsquatches" and leaf-face pareidolia? Why is every DNA test done on any piece of bigfoot hair, scat, or blood declared inconclusive, contaminated, or determined otherwise not fit for scientific review? Why do so many bigfoot researchers, once respected, eventually get tied to hoaxes, faked evidence, or other sketchy scams?

Something very, very strange is going on, beyond giant hairy apemen. Something that often reaches beyond the woods and right into the lives of witnesses and researchers involved in this subject. A grand government conspiracy is often suggested. Certain secret agencies within the government, it is said, *know* about these creatures. They just don't want *us* to know about them. Or they don't want us to know *they* know about them. Or some combination of these things. This could be the case, but again, *WHY?* The idea that it would somehow impact the logging industry if these creatures were confirmed is laughable. *NOTHING* stops the great wheels of capitalism for long - history shows this repeatedly. The Peach Bottom Atomic Power Station was built right on the banks of the Susquehanna River which feeds directly into the incredibly important and ecologically sensitive Chesapeake Bay watershed. This is a perfect example of economic "progress" taking precedent over ecological concerns, and it falls directly within the area of which I write about in this article! So, again, if the government knows about these creatures, which may be the case, why are they keeping it a secret?

Like it or not, there is something weird attached to the bigfoot phenomenon. Joshua Cutchin, a friend and Fortean author himself, has said to me on multiple occasions, concerning bigfoot and similar topics: "Consider the company these things keep." It is simple, but exceptional advice. A glance above will show, along with sightings of hair-covered giants, there are tales of haunted houses; headless ghosts; spirit contact and automatic writing; unidentified shadowy things; fairy rings; UFOs, will-o-the-wisps, and other mystery lights; leprechauns; and even buried pirate treasure all within this same area of about 8 square miles, in one corner of York County, Pennsylvania. Something strange is happening here. You can toss out some of these things as coincidence, but will you refuse to consider *any* of them? Yes, people are seeing bigfoot here - and have been seeing them for a very long time, but look at the company these creatures keep.

Starting with Nemiah and Mary Cooper's sighting - the bucket-sized something that rises to a much bigger height is easy to explain. Many bigfoot witnesses have reported seeing the creatures spring upright from a prone position. The strangeness kicks in when they describe the immense size of the creature, 12 to 15 feet tall and 6 or 7 feet wide is absolutely massive, even by bigfoot standards. It's possible that the witnesses overestimated the size of the creature - they wouldn't have had any reference for what was approaching them in the darkness. "Bigfoot" was not part of popular culture at the time. Most of the newspaper reports from the time, if the Coopers had even read them, report the creatures as "wild men" - a name that in no way would prepare someone for seeing a bigfoot creature. I find it curious as well that the Cooper party throws stones at the creature - an oft-documented bigfoot behavior.

The reports of shadowy undefined figures in the different stories above *may* be explained as bigfoot. Likewise, bigfoot may have been the reason travelers were told to avoid the African-American cemetery. The creatures have been seen frequenting rural graveyards. The horses that stopped at a certain point by the McConkey Mansion - these too could have sensed bigfoot creatures and refused to move on - this has been reported in conjunction with other bigfoot sightings. The howls and screams reported throughout the area - those were certainly bigfoot, right? Possibly.

I do believe that bigfoot or other cryptid creatures may be a possible explanation for many areas reported to be haunted. This was what I found when I researched and explored the sighting reports of another area of strangeness in York County, Toad Road. Because the area was reportedly haunted, when witnesses reported things stalking them, peeking from behind trees, horrible screams in the night, and dark shadowy figures pacing them in the woods, these things were being reported as ghosts. The man who was attacked by something large, bipedal, and hair-covered on Toad Road would beg to differ.

However, consider the notion that ghosts may be a possible explanation for many bigfoot encounters. I am thinking of things like rocks or other objects being thrown by unseen things. Disembodied screams. Knocking sounds. The feelings of intense fear people often report. Bad smells. All of these things are sometimes reported in conjunction with poltergeist activity. The difference is the hauntings usually happen inside a structure.

It is worth noting not every suspected bigfoot print found in the Delta / Peach Bottom area was of the three-toed variety, but many were. The three-toed tracks have been documented elsewhere - Stan Gordon recorded many in western Pennsylvania, and at least some of the tracks found around Boggy Creek were of the three-toed variety. I've inspected casts of the three-toed tracks found near Delta and they are indeed odd. It's possible we are looking at some kind of genetic defect: five toes, through syndactyly or some other process, forged into the appearance of three. Some people have suggested inbreeding, but this tends to cause more digits, not fewer, so it seems unlikely. Whatever we are looking at, unless this one three-toed bigfoot creature made it's way from Fouke, Arkansas up through western Pennsylvania and over to south-central Pennsylvania and northern Maryland, we are seeing multiple creatures with the same attributes or defects. Three big, weird toes on a creature that is already not supposed to exist.

Then we are left with these *other* things. Ghosts, spiritualists contacting the dead, leprechauns, and perhaps most troubling of all for the bigfoot enthusiast wanting to avoid "woo" - those pesky mystery lights. Anyone researching bigfoot sightings long enough is bound to run into reports of these mystery lights. Will-o-the-wisps and UFOs are the most commonly reported around the same time and place as bigfoot sightings. These lights are not always reported, and they are not even reported in conjunction with *most* bigfoot sightings - but they are reported together often enough where it seems willfully ignorant not to at least note their appearance. Look at the company these things keep.

I am not suggesting bigfoot is riding around in UFOs; that aliens are dropping genetically modified hairy ape-men off on our planet; or that bigfoot play catch with will-o-the wisp lights. I don't know why these sightings are happening in relatively the same time and place. It could be coincidence - but if so, how strange a coincidence! It could be that whatever conditions are favorable for a bigfoot sighting just happen to be favorable to mystery lights as well.

How rare is it to see a bigfoot, and how rare to see a UFO? Now what are the chances that both will be seen in the same general area within a few hours or even days? And yet we get these reports with some frequency. It happened in Delta in 1978. Stan Gordon recorded many, many reports of bigfoots in relative conjunction with UFOs (and more than one report where both UFOs and bigfoot creatures were seen at the same time). I often say, half-jokingly (but only half): find me a bigfoot sighting in Pennsylvania and I will find you a UFO sighting in the same general area and within a few days. This is an exaggeration, of course, but there is more than a grain of truth to the joke.

Talk to bigfoot witnesses for any length of time and something odder than the idea of an undiscovered wood ape is bound to surface. After the trackway of prints appeared on the Hilsmeier farm, Allen Hilsmeier himself became an active bigfoot researcher, starting a local group called Bigfoot Investigations. Mr. Hilsmeier is a down to earth fellow, and believes the creatures to be nothing more than highly elusive, extremely rare, but otherwise wholly natural animals. There is no "woo" about Mr. Hilsmeier. However, he stopped his Bigfoot Investigations organization shortly after he started it. The reason: he was to running into too many "crazy" people and stories.

When we discussed the trackway he and his sons found in 1978, Mr. Hilsmeier said to me: "Do you know these things are aware of their tracks?" "What makes you say that?" I asked. He replied: "Those tracks just stopped in the middle of a field - the creature had to back track in it's own steps." I have heard this explanation many times, reasoning why bigfoot trackways sometimes seem to just stop. Other explanations I've seen are that the creatures made some kind of superhuman jump and the next set of tracks was so impossibly far away and to one side or the other that whoever was following the trackway never found the continuing footprints.

Both explanations are possible. It seems to me, however that a creature walking backward in its own tracks - especially a big heavy creature with a long stride and really big feet - is bound to mess up those tracks beyond recognition. In fact, if the desire was to confuse anyone who might follow the footprints as to which way the creature went, there would be some advantage to having a messed up, confusing trackway. Instead we must imagine a great heavy ape-man delicately tip-toeing backward through each step, over miles of trackway, so as not to smudge his footprints and fool some humans who may or may not ever find the tracks anyway. Likewise, we must imagine a huge leap with no real evidence of weight shifting or smeared footprints in those last tracks as the pressure of such a jump would require - a delicate sideways leap of such great distance that it throws off any trackers, human or canine - and it only *looks* like the trackway ended in the middle of a field. Again, both explanations are possible, but it's a long way to go to keep away the "woo." Has anyone actually observed the creatures doing these things?

It's ok not to have answers. The answer doesn't have to be "woo," just because we don't understand how or why these strange things are happening. So many people turn to these really wild explanations - the verbal equivalent of Rube Goldberg devices for explaining bigfoot behavior. Multiplying unnecessarily conjecture after conjecture in order to offer some kind of "reasonable" explanation science will accept when science hasn't accepted the word of real and respected scientists on this subject (those few that do speak out on the reality of bigfoot creatures).

There is no such thing as a bigfoot expert. We're all just wandering around in the dark, looking for an 8-foot tall ape-man, and looking for answers. Your guess is as good as mine, but don't pretend it's anything more than a guess until we know - *really* know - what these things are. If you choose to ignore all the other weirdness that goes along with bigfoot, that is your prerogative, but I cannot ignore it. Somehow bigfoot fits into this puzzle of strangeness along with ghosts, mystery lights, and all of the attendant oddities. If it doesn't - if someone rolls a bigfoot body into a lab one day, or proves conclusively, one way or another, that these things are nothing more than natural animals - I will be the first to say: I was wrong. I am not holding my breath waiting for that day. Disclosure is not forthcoming. Not from scientists. Not from the government. Not from aliens holding a press conference. Not from the BFRO or any of the hundreds of other bigfoot research groups that have sprung up across the country, their initials proudly emblazoned across t-shirts and baseball caps.

Please prove me wrong! It will be much easier that way. It's much easier to talk about an undiscovered primate or a relict hominid than an "I don't know." Because, in the end, that is what I have to tell people: I don't know what bigfoot creatures are. I don't know why they are being seen so often in this one small section of York County. I absolutely believe people are seeing them. I believe they are leaving footprints, scat and hair behind. I believe they are killing pets and livestock. I believe they attack and even kill humans on occasion. I also believe there is something very, very strange about these creatures. We have been seeing them since the dawn of time, across the planet, and our answers come down to folklore and guesses. Just because I don't know, doesn't mean I have to give up the search or stop trying to understand.

I spend a lot of time in the Delta / Peach Bottom area. Besides the beautiful hiking, my interest in bigfoot keeps drawing me back, searching and wondering. I visited Mt. Nebo church and found Nemiah Cooper's grave. I've made the trip from Slate Hill to Cooper Road many times. I've visited the Hilsmeier farm and walked the trail beside Muddy Creek.

In the spring of 2017, I parked my jeep along Cooper Road and walked the road along the Michael Run (this stream would have been known as Rock Run in Nemiah Cooper's time). At the bridge where Cooper Road crosses Michael Run I found something in the hard-packed mud along the roadside. It looked to be a large footprint, about 15 inches in length. It wasn't perfectly defined. I couldn't make out individual toes or other details. It just looked very much like a large, bare, humanoid footprint. I tried to make an impression in the packed mud and, even when jumping, hardly left a mark. Looking in the direction the track came from, there was a steep bank leading up into the woods. This bank was covered with dry leaves, and it was obvious something large had made its way down the bank, leaving a disturbed wake of leaves in its path. Following the direction the track pointed, in the middle of the road, in the middle of the bridge, there was a large pile of scat. I grew up on a farm and I am familiar with horse and cow scat - this pile was neither of those. Nor did it seem to be bear scat. Then again, it didn't look like *human* feces, as bigfoot scat has often been reported to appear.

Both scat and footprint were inconclusive. I would expect nothing more or less.

Sources:

Altman, Eric. Bigfoot Sighting Report Files.

BFRO Report #3572 (www.bfro.net)

Chance, Bob. *Earthline.* (Coachwhip Publications, 2008)

Chance, Bob. Bigfoot Sighting Report Files.

The Delta Herald

"A Ghost Story", The Delta Herald (Delta, PA), November 5, 1886.

The Delta-Herald Times

"Wiley Hollow", *The Delta-Herald Times* (Delta, PA), January 19, 1912.

Gordon, Stan. *Silent Invasion: The Pennsylvania UFO-Bigfoot Casebook.* (Stan Gordon, 2010)

Renner, Timothy. *Beyond the Seventh Gate.* (Dark Holler Arts, 2016)

Renner, Timothy. *Bigfoot in Pennsylvania.* (Dark Holler Arts, 2017)

Treasured Recipes, Friends of the Welsh Cottages, 2008

Wolfe, Maggie Ann. *Was Peach Bottom Mansion Haunted* (article posted at the Old Line Museum, Delta Pennsylvania)

York Daily Record

"Bigfoot 'Wild Man of Woods' Roams County. *York Daily Record* (York, PA), February 23, 1978.

"Bigfoot: Baltimore Trucker Sees Seven-Foot 'Whopper' Near Atomic Plant". *York Daily Record* (York, PA), March 7, 1978.

Nick Redfern at Shepherd's Monument (photo by author)

The "Demon" Bigfoot of the U.K.

by Nick Redfern

Situated near to the picturesque, ancient hamlet of Milford, Staffordshire, England, Shugborough Hall is both a large and renowned country house that serves as the ancestral home of the Earls of the city of Lichfield. And its spacious grounds are connected to the nearby village of Great Haywood by the Essex Bridge, which was built during the Middle-Ages. Around 1750, the hall was greatly enlarged, and then yet again at the beginning of the 1800s. Today, Shugborough Hall is open to the general public and has a working farm museum that dates back to 1805, and which is complete with a watermill, kitchens and a dairy.

Interestingly, the grounds of Shugborough Hall are also home to something known as the Shepherd's Monument, upon which can be found a very strange and baffling inscription, and one which, many students of the puzzle believe, contains a secret code that identifies the alleged resting place of none other than the legendary Holy Grail. The Shepherd's Monument is not the only such construction of note on the grounds of the sprawling old hall: The Tower of Winds, the Cat's Monument, and the Doric Temple also have pride of place. But, get this: The thick and mysterious woods that surround Shugborough Hall are said to be the domain of nothing less than a diabolical, hairy wild man, or perhaps even several.

So the controversial story goes, at some point in the early to mid-part of 1981, distinctly strange events took place late at night in the finely landscaped grounds of Shugborough Hall. On no less than five occasions – and specifically between February and June of that year – an undisclosed number of the many geese and ducks that frequented the pleasant waters that surround the hall were found brutally decapitated, and with their lifeless bodies laid out in what one employee of the Shugborough estate described concisely and notably as resembling "a witchcraft ceremony." Precisely how the man knew what "a witchcraft ceremony" involving decapitated water-fowl might look like, however, is pretty much anybody's guess. And far more was to come. All of it was much, much worse.

Shugborough Hall (photo by author)

On at least two occasions strange, loud, guttural noises were heard coming from one particular tree-shrouded area of the spacious grounds, and a large, hairy, man-like thing was observed by a shocked employee bounding at very high speed across the lawns long after the sun had gone down - and specifically heading in the direction of the winding waters that continue to run throughout the Shugborough Hall estate to this very day. Somewhat significantly, the very same employee recalled hearing a loud splashing noise in the immediate aftermath of the sighting, which suggested strongly that the creature had actually propelled itself deep into the heart of those very same, darkened waters.

One of those willing to discuss certain, salient aspects of the above – albeit from the promised safety and camouflage of a thick veil of secrecy and anonymity – is a now-elderly man who was employed to look after the lawns at Shugborough Hall from the late 1970s to the early 1980s. To this day he alludes to semi-veiled warnings made by senior staff at the hall at the time in question that went something very much along these lines: "Do not to talk about the killings, the beheadings, the rites and the rituals. And most certainly do not discuss with anyone the sightings of the wild, hairy man-beast."

Nevertheless, despite the ominous order of complete silence, the man does, at least, confirm that a decision was taken at the very highest level "not to report anything to the police," and he further asserts that "everything" was dealt with strictly in-house; aside, that is, from a visit by a local veterinarian whose services were occasionally used to treat the pet animals that lived at the hall, and who reportedly made a detailed examination of the dead water-fowl. Precisely what the results of that examination were, we unfortunately do not know, and probably never will.

The same source has been able to fill in the blanks relative to several other aspects of the story, however: Namely, (A) that the man-beast seen running wildly in the grounds exuded a foul smell that was somewhat akin to that of rotting vegetation; (B) that not a single one of the dead birds appeared to have put up a fight before decapitation (for example, there were no large piles of feathers laying around, no blood, and the birds looked to have been cleanly-cut and not torn open); and (C) that he had heard, from a colleague and friend, of "something like this happening here once before, in the 1960s, with a big monkey running around."

Some twenty years ago or more now, I paid a visit to Shugborough Hall and had a brief opportunity to chat with a handful of the employees about the legend of the hairy wild man said to have been in their very midst, all those years earlier. Although none of them had any personal awareness of the story (which is not at all surprising, given that the chief events took place a decade and a half before I even thought about engaging them in conversation) they did admit to finding the whole thing very intriguing, and eventually related to me a series of entertainingly paranormal tales of various unknown entities said to haunt Shugborough Hall. Although, it must be said that these were all of a distinctly ghostly and spectral nature – of the typical "grey lady" and "hooded monk" variety - and most certainly not of a hairy and Bigfoot-like style.

While a direct connection to the presence of the Shugborough man-beast could never be firmly proved, one of the employees did recall a weird event that had supposedly occurred around four years previous to my visit. In this case, a horse had apparently been violently slashed on its back legs in a fashion that looked suspiciously like the work of a wild animal, such as a "big cat." Unfortunately, there were no more relevant details available; and so, therefore, I could do very little more than merely log the story for posterity, and in the event that further corroborating data might ultimately one day surface. To my lasting regret, it never has. But, since then, another account has surfaced that does add to the overall mystery, even though it does not relate to the events of the 1960s or the early 1980s.

In 2004, a further encounter with the elusive, hairy wild man occurred. The location was the road that runs from the hamlet of Milford to Shugborough Hall. And, in this case, the witness had impeccable credentials. She was a policewoman who, while on duty with a colleague on the night in question, was routinely patrolling the coiling old roads that run through the woods, and which surround the vast Shugborough estate. It was not long before midnight – yes, the veritable witching hour itself, no less - when both she and her partner were shocked by the sight of a strange beast that bounded across the road, only a short distance in front of them, and headed towards the expansive fields that dominate the old, historic hall.

In a 2006 off the record interview, the officer described to me the animal as being human-like in shape, an estimated, and incredible, eight and a half feet in height, covered in dark hair, but looking practically emaciated and near-anorexic in appearance. Her amazed colleague, who was driving, slammed on the brakes and brought the car to a screeching halt in the middle of the moonlit road. The shocked pair looked at each other for a moment; then, on regaining their composure they elected to do absolutely nothing.

No-one would believe their story, the officer stated to me. They would likely receive nothing more than ridicule and endless jokes and jibes from their colleagues if they dared speak even a single word of the night's events. And, in addition to that, what purpose would it really serve to alert the staff at Shugborough Hall to the possibility that a creature acutely akin to Bigfoot was prowling around the area? Absolutely no purpose at all, they both quickly and quietly – and, perhaps, reasonably - concluded.

This self-imposed silence on the part of the pair begs an intriguing question: How many other people have had an up close and personal encounter with the monster of Shugborough Hall, but have also elected to say nothing, for fear of similar ridicule and hoots of derision? Maybe the number is none or but just a scant few. Perhaps, however, it runs to dozens; we may never really know the answer to that one.

There is one, final point worth noting with regard to the saga of the monster of Shugborough Hall. And it's a potentially highly significant point, too. "Shug" – as in Shugborough - is an ancient English term derived from an even older Anglo-Saxon word, "scucca," which means...demon. Shugborough: The borough of the demon. How very, very appropriate. And, that term, "Shug," pops up in other cases concerning what we might term the "British Bigfoot."

Any mention of the mysterious locale that is Rendlesham Forest, Suffolk inevitably conjures up strange and surreal images of the famous, alleged UFO landing within the forest in the latter part of December 1980 – a startling event witnessed by numerous United States Air Force personnel stationed at a nearby military base, Royal Air Force Bentwaters. The bizarre affair has been the subject of a considerable number of books, numerous television shows, several investigations by military and governmental bodies, and unrelenting deep debate. Reports of strange lights, of small alien-like creatures seen deep within the heart of the woods, and of high-level cover-ups and sinister conspiracies, are all key ingredients of the case that has, for many, justifiably become known as the "British Roswell."

More than three decades on, the events in question continue to provoke intense debate and controversy, with some believing that extraterrestrials really did land on British soil on that fateful night, or as some believe, across the course of several nights. Others hold the view that everything can be attributed to mistaken identity (of a nearby lighthouse, no less!), while some prefer the theory that a dark and dubious military experiment, and subsequent disastrous mishap, may have been to blame for all of the fuss. More than thirty years on, the debate continues to rage, and doubtless it will continue to rage for many more years to come.

As for the forest itself, it covers an area that is around 1,500 hectares in size and can be found in Suffolk's coastal belt known as the Sandlings. It is comprised of large, coniferous trees, as well as heath land and wet land areas, and is home to the badger, the fox, the red deer, the roe deer and the fallow deer. According to some people, however, Rendlesham Forest is home to far weirder things, too. Maybe, even, a strange form of British Bigfoot.

Rendlesham Forest, as well as the Suffolk locales of West Wratting and Balsham, is reportedly home to something equally as strange – maybe even far more so – than a vehicle and creatures from another world. It is a beast that, locally, has come to be known as the Shug Monkey. Described as being a bizarre combination of giant dog, muscular bear, and large ape, the creature is said to take its name from either (A) that old English word – scucca – which means demon, and which, as we have seen already, also has a link to the naming of Shugborough Hall, Staffordshire; or (B) an old east-coast term – Shucky or Shuck – that translates, into modern day terminology, as hairy or shaggy. Maybe the name is even born out of a curious melding of both terms. But, whatever the true nature of the name applied to the foul, hairy entity, its presence in the woods of Suffolk is enough to strike deep terror into the hearts of those souls unfortunate enough to have crossed its path – which is something to which Sam Holland most definitely attested to.

Shortly after New Year's Day in 1956, Holland was walking through the Suffolk countryside with his spaniel dog, Harry, when he was horrified to see a bizarre-looking creature come looming out of the trees some forty feet in front of him. It walked upon four huge, muscular legs – 'like a lion's' – and its thick fur coat was both black and glossy. Incredibly, said Holland, the animal was easily ten feet in length, and so could not be considered anything even remotely resembling a domestic animal, or a known wild beast of the British Isles.

Holland, in a panicked state, thought for a moment that perhaps the animal was an exotic big cat that had escaped from a zoo or private estate; that is until it turned in his direction and he was finally able to see its terrible, frowning face. Likening it to that of nothing less than a silver-back gorilla, Holland said that the monstrous creature possessed a huge neck, intelligent-looking eyes, widely flaring nostrils, and immense, powerful jaws of a bone-crushing nature. For a moment or two, the animal looked intently at Holland and his whimpering little dog. Then, seemingly having lost any and all interest in the pair, the gorilla-faced nightmare simply continued on its way and into the depths of the surrounding undergrowth. Holland would later explain that the creature looked like a strange combination of ape, dog, bear, lion and rhinoceros. An absolute chimera of the highest order, one might be very inclined to say.

Needless to say, the British Isles are not home to any such animal that even remotely resembles the beast that Sam Holland says he stumbled upon all those years ago. In fact, it's fair to say that nowhere on the entire planet does such a creature dwell. Yet, Holland was adamant that his description of the monstrous entity and his recollections of the day in question are utterly accurate in each and every respect. Right up until the time of his death, Holland believed that whatever the true nature of the beast he had the distinct misfortune to run into more than half a century ago, it was unquestionably paranormal rather than physical in origin. But from where, precisely, he admittedly has no idea whatsoever.

Jon Downes – of the U.K.-based Center for Fortean Zoology - has a tantalizing tale to tell, too, of Rendlesham Forest's most monstrous inhabitant, the Shug Monkey: 'An ex-girlfriend of mine - an East Anglian paranormal researcher - was in possession of some video-tape which showed the paw print of some huge animal like that of a cat or a dog, but far bigger and with strange flattened finger nails rather than claws. She thought that it was a print from an alien big cat of some description, but my immediate thought was of the semi-mystical "Shug Monkey." When I later found that my friend and colleague, Jan Scarff, who was brought up in the vicinity of the air bases, also knew about the so-called "Shug Monkey" I became even more interested, and I have been collecting reports for some years.'

Moving on…

According to a Glasgow, Scotland electrician named Danny Thomas, on a particular evening in January 1879, his great-great-grandfather, who had apparently suffered from some form of severe mental affliction, committed suicide by hurling himself off Scotland's Tay Bridge, and right into the harsh depths of Dundee's Firth of Tay. But there is much more to come right now: In the immediate days that followed the family's tragic loss, ominous reports began to quietly circulate within the close-knit confines of the neighborhood of a shaggy-haired man-beast that was seen roaming the Tay Bridge late at night, and that came to be known locally as the Shuggy – a term that instantly evokes thoughts of Rendlesham Forest's Shug Monkey and the Bigfoot-infested grounds around Shugborough Hall, Staffordshire.

As far as the known data are concerned, at least, the story goes like this: Almost two miles in length and carrying a single rail track, the bridge – completed in February 1878 to the plans of Sir Thomas Bouch – was the longest in the world at that time. Proposals for such a bridge dated back to 1854, and its foundation stone had been laid with ceremony on July 22, 1871. The first engine duly crossed the bridge on September 22, 1877, and the bridge was officially opened by Queen Victoria on June 1, 1878. Ulysses S. Grant worded it correctly when he commented that it was "a big bridge for a small city." But that situation soon changed – and most definitely not for the better.

Tay Bridge (photo by author)

It was an appropriately dark and stormy night on December 28, 1879 when, at around 7.15 p.m., and as a veritable storm of truly deluge-style proportions was blowing right down the length of the estuary, the central navigation spans of the Tay Bridge collapsed and plummeted into the Firth of Tay – taking with them a train and six carriages that resulted in no less than seventy-five untimely and tragic deaths. Legend and urban-myth that still circulates in Dundee to this very day holds that - had illness not intervened - none other than Karl Marx himself would have been aboard the doomed train.

A Court of Inquiry set up at the time decided that: '...the fall of the bridge was occasioned by the insufficiency of the cross bracing and its fastenings to sustain the force of the gale'. Had the wind-bracing been properly concluded, said the Court, the bridge might very well have withstood the intense battering of the mighty storm. Regardless of the real nature of the tragedy, however, the trail of death was still far from over. Plans were duly made for a new bridge to be built – according to the designs of one William Henry Barlow. The first stone was laid on July 6, 1883; and, by the time of its completion, no less than fourteen of the construction workers were dead, all from a variety of accidents.

It must be said that Danny Thomas was most definitely not an adherent of the theory that the Tay Bridge disaster could be attributed to something as down to earth as the stormy and relentless British weather. No: It was his firm belief that the dark and sinister forces of the Shuggy were at work on that most tragic of all nights. Moreover, Danny was of the opinion that the precise cause of the Tay Bridge disaster of December 1879 was his great-great-grandfather; returned, after his January 1879 death, to our plane of existence in the spectral form of some vile man-beast that haunted the darkened corners of the bridge – positively oozing negative energy and creating an atmosphere of death, doom, tragedy and decay as it did so.

In conclusion, what can we say for sure about this very curious state of affairs? The fact is that it's impossible for a colony (or multiple colonies) of giant, Bigfoot-type creatures to exist in a nation the small size of the U.K. and not be caught, photographed, or killed. Yet, people see them – and very credible people, too. Undeniably, we are dealing with something that is not flesh and blood in nature – at least, not in the way we would describe a living creature.

The people of earlier times clearly had a greater understanding and knowledge of the British beasts than we do today. Hence the reason why we see such hairy hominids in the U.K. described as being "demonic" in nature. There can be little doubt (if any) that the terms "Shug," "Shuggy," "Shuck," "Scucca" and "Shucky" all have one, original point of origin. Whether that means they are literal demons – or baffling entities from realms or dimensions beyond ours – very much depends on your personal perspectives and belief-systems. Of only one thing can we be truly sure: the terrible Shug-beast is among us and has been for a very long time.

Sources:

Downes, Jonathan. *Monster Hunter: In Search of Unknown Beasts at Home and Abroad.* Woolsery, U.K.: CFZ Press, 2004.

Lockley, Mike. "200-year-old mystery of Shugborough Code 'solved.'"

https://www.birminghampost.co.uk/news/regional-affairs/200-year-old-mystery-shugborough-code-solved-8319385. December 21, 2014.

"Shug Monkey." http://cryptidz.wikia.com/wiki/Shug_Monkey.

"The Tay Bridge Disaster." http://taybridgedisaster.co.uk/.

Nick Redfern is the author of many books, including *The Black Diary, Men in Black, Women in Black, Shapeshifters and The Monster Book.* He can be reached at his blog, "World of Whatever," at http://nickredfernfortean.blogspot.com

Massive Florida track find (photo by author)

The Florida Skunk Ape

by Robert Robinson

When people think about a large hairy bipedal ape prowling around the woods, they immediately think of the legendary creature, Bigfoot. Most people do not know that in the southeastern part of the U.S. lives a cryptid animal not unlike Bigfoot. It goes by many names, but the most popular name is the Skunk Ape. Believe it or not, Florida is ranked in the top five states for large, hairy unidentified primate sightings.

The Skunk Ape is probably the most famous of all the legends in the Sunshine State. It is reported to look a lot like its western cousin, all covered with dark brown hair, extremely muscular and a cross between an ape and human. Witnesses report the Skunk Ape is about eight-feet tall and weighs 200 to 300 pounds, characterized by the foul odor this cryptid emits. This smell is often described as being similar to rotten eggs or a wet canine, hence the name "Skunk Ape." The only real difference is the Skunk Ape is quite fond of making its home in the swamplands of Florida, whereas Bigfoot likes the mountains and forests.

The Bigfoot Field Research Organization has over two hundred and eighty-three sightings recorded on their website in Florida alone. The creature was reported in all parts of Florida, from up in the panhandle to the central area not far from the Orlando attractions, and even within an area close to Cape Kennedy.

Stories of this creature started when the early settlers came to

Florida and reported a strange primate-like creature prowling the forests and swamps with its nauseous smell. Prior to western incursion, the native Seminoles have a long history of this creature and refer to it as Esti Capcaki (Cannibal Giant). This cryptid creature is also known as the swamp cabbage man, swamp ape, stink ape, Florida Bigfoot, Myakka ape, Swampsquatch, and Myakka skunk ape; one town in Florida even calls it the Bardin Booger. Newspapers have referred to it as the "Wild Man" or the Everglades Ape. The Yeti Research Society and Researcher Ramona Clarke Hibbner referred to it in her reports as a Yeti.

The name Skunk Ape made the media attention in Florida when amateur archeologist HC Osborn, along with four other associates observed a seven-foot-tall primate, covered in reddish hair, in the area known as the Big Cypress Swamp in 1971. When interviewed by the press Osborn stated the animal he saw was a Skunk Ape, and the name has stuck with the media as the primary moniker ever since.

Sightings of these elusive cryptids range in the hundreds. Unfortunately, some sightings go undocumented by hunters and hikers, not wishing to endure ridicule. The Skunk Ape reports cover virtually every part of Florida except the Keys

The first recorded sighting of an unknown primate in Florida was 1818 at Apalachicola, described as a 5ft tall baboon. As a side note, the first zoo and circus in the state were not opened until 1927.

The second recorded sighting was in 1929 in the Okefenokee Swamp, near the Georgia border. The story goes that two hunters along with a Native American guide left the settlement and journeyed down from Georgia into Florida. As they explored the very heart of the swamp, they made a startling discovery of gigantic footprints. Their Indian guide told them that giant cannibals were said to prowl the swamplands. Not wanting to see what made the tracks, they quickly retreated out of the swamp, back to their settlement.

Upon their return to their settlement, they related to their friends and neighbors what they had seen. This excited the curiosity of other hunters in the settlement. Nine hunters to include one of the hunters from the original party, then went back into the swamp, to search for what made the footprints. As the men made camp for the night, they began to hear screams coming from the swamp. They could also hear something large circling their camp. The men held their rifles at the ready. Then it went deathly quiet. The men shaking with their guns pointed into the darkness.

Suddenly a large creature leaped out of the bush and rushed the hunting party. The men started firing at the gigantic beast as it tore at them. Before the animal finally fell to the ground, five of the hunters lay dead with their heads literally screwed from their bodies. As the creature lay writhing and screaming, the survivors approached it to make a closer inspection. The huge hairy beast measured in at thirteen feet from head to toe.

With the creature screaming the hunters fled the swamp, leaving their dead comrades where they had fallen. While there is some debate if the story really happened, newspapers later reported that people living in Ware County on the margins of the Okefenokee Swamp clearly believed it and never set foot in that area again.

This is one of the rare sightings where the animal actually attacked humans. Some folklorists say the creature that attacked the hunters was a giant bear, while others say it is something else entirely. For the record, there are no giant bears in Florida or Georgia.

The third recorded sighting of a large primate-like animal occurred in the winter of 1883-1884, which was originally reported as a Wild Man, appeared at Ocheesee Pond, a large wetland covering nearly nine square miles in southeastern Jackson County. Located below Grand Ridge and Sneads in the southeast corner of Jackson County, Ocheesee Pond was a focal point for early settlers. The pond is covered by a vast cypress swamp, although there are some stretches of open water - most notably its southern arm. The strange human-like creature was often spotted roaming the swamps or swimming from place to place.

As more sightings occurred in the remote area, the local residents - many of them former Confederate soldiers - met and launched an expedition to capture the Wild Man of Ocheesee Pond. In August of 1884, they succeeded! It was reported his body was covered in thick hair, but the captors believed he was a human who had probably escaped from an asylum. No asylum reported such an odd escapee, however, and the captors became even more baffled by the Wild Man. The account tells of the strange beast being sent to Tallahassee and then back to Chattahoochee after scientists could not identify it. Unfortunately, that is where the report ends. Newspapers at the time were silent on the eventual fate of the Ocheesee Pond Wild Man.

The first group to investigate reports on the Skunk ape were the Yeti Research Society headquartered in St. Petersburg started in 1973 by L Frank Hudson and Gordon Prescott. The group would actively send investigators out to interview witnesses and conduct an investigation at the sighting locations. The Yeti Research Society received sighting reports from Florida and around the US and published a monthly newsletter of the various sightings. The group disbanded in 1975, but Gordon Prescott continued investigating reported sightings.

A capture of a Yeti was reported in Arcadia, Florida in 1934, according to Prescott. A Yeti was destroying cattle, and ranchers, fed up with the nuisance, tracked the Yeti - a female - and captured it. Not knowing what else to do with the thing, the ranchers locked it up in the Arcadia jail, but that plan lasted only a month. The other prisoners and jailers couldn't tolerate the smell - similar to rotten eggs - nor the sound of the thing for longer than that, so the ranchers supposedly took the Yeti back to where they found it and set it free. A call to the Arcadia historic society revealed that most of the newspapers records from that time period were not maintained, and are no longer available. Arcadia is located right next to Myakka National Forest, which is a hotbed of Skunk Ape sightings.

Another group from the 70's was Yeti Evaluation and Technological Investigators started in 1974 by George Kelly. The group was a splinter group of the Yeti Research Society, and made its headquarters at the Luck K ranch, in Brooksville, FL, where several Skunk Ape sightings had occurred.

The most notable investigator and member of both the Yeti Research Society and the Yeti Evaluation and Technological Investigators was Ramone Clarke Hibbner. Having first seen it in Brooksville, Ramone moved from Jacksonville to Brooksville and started recording and investigating the numerous sightings. From the 1950's to her untimely death in 1997, she recorded sightings not only in Florida, but in Georgia, Alabama and Tennessee. It should be noted Ramone did not like the name Skunk Ape and referred to the cryptid as a Yeti. Ramone also made a correlation of UFO and Bigfoot sightings after she and her husband Duane observed both a UFO and then shortly later a large hairy creature within the same area.

Noted Bigfoot Researcher John Green in his 1978 book

"Sasquatch; Apes Among Us," goes over some of the sightings in Florida. In the beginning John seemed skeptical of a large primate type creature in Florida, due to the states size and the number of reports. Toward the end he seemed to come to the realization that not only are people truly seeing this cryptid, but that there is able land for this animal to remain hidden. He felt that as Florida continued to grow and develop, the viable habitat for such a creature would noticeably dwindle and their numbers would naturally diminish. Green inherited the bulk of Ramone's research and sightings.

Following are some sightings and accounts from different periods and regions of Florida. While there are hundreds of reported sightings, I picked what I felt to be some of the more interesting ones. You will note that the Everglades and the Green Swamp locations will come up numerous times in these accounts. These areas even today are still relatively undeveloped. The sightings are arranged in chronological order by date.

After the national release of Roger Patterson's infamous film clip of a Bigfoot in California in 1967, a wave of Bigfoot reports emerged in Florida. While Skunk Ape sightings were reported well before the film caught national attention, the residents of Florida pretty much thought they were dealing with an escaped primate from a zoo or a wild man. With the Patterson film, residents revealed that they, too had a Bigfoot of their own prowling the swamplands of the Sunshine State.

HC Osborn reported his sighting of a seven-foot-tall primate, covered in reddish hair, in the Big Cypress Swamp in 1971, near a trailer park on the edge of the Everglades. The next reported sighting happened two weeks after Mr. Osborn's, when two boys saw two, large hairy ape-type creatures on their patio. The Broward County rabies control office was called and investigator Henry Ring, after interviewing the boys found not only large foot and knuckle prints, but found their tale was apparently just the tip of the iceberg. Further investigation revealed most if not all the trailer park residents had heard and seen a large ape like creature roaming outside their trailers at night. Most of the residents said they would hear it growling outside, and when they went out to investigate, would hear it fleeing into the nearby swamps.

One resident, a Mrs. Robert King, said she heard her dog barking outside. She opened the door and walked on to her patio to find two large hairy creatures staring at her. She immediately fled back inside, but not without getting a good look at the creature. Mrs. King described the creature as five-foot-high with grayish hair, large teeth, and long arms. She also noted the animal was covered in large sores.

Another resident reported that her young daughter went out onto the patio and saw a large hairy ape standing next to the swamp watching her. She screamed, and her brother came out to see not only creatures, but a second one that emerged from the swamps and stood next to the other one. The boy immediately started yelling and screaming at the creatures, which then ran into a nearby orange grove. The resident declined to give her name or allow her children to be interviewed.

Another resident, Mrs. Gladys Scarpulla stated that she and her family heard the animal outside her trailer grunting and groaning at night, causing many sleepless nights.

Noting the multiple sightings in this particular area, Ring contacted the police and discovered there were sightings of this creature going back for over a year. Ring also added that at first he thought the whole thing was a hoax, but seeing how scared the residents were, convinced him that something mysterious was prowling around the trailer park.

In Aug. 1971, Ring, with a fifteen-man posse went out into the swamp, armed with guns and nets to search for the creatures. They conducted their search for two days. While they did find tracks and heard something large moving around, they did not find the elusive Skunk Ape.

One account had the newspapers claiming South Florida got hit with Skunk Ape fever in 1974. Richard Lee Smith was driving home at 12:40 am on 9 Jan, when he sideswiped an eight foot hairy creature with his Cadillac on Hollywood Boulevard. He then went and filed a report with the Florida Highway Patrol. A couple hours later Hialeah Garden Police Officer Robert Holmeyer saw the creature thrashing off into the underbrush, about five miles south of where Smith had his encounter. Later investigation found only a shredded hollyberry tree, but the account ignited a slew of more accounts.

In May 1975 an unusual report came out of Central Florida. This happened in the town of Bushnell, about an hour west of Orlando. The authorities were combing the Green Swamp, in search of a Taiwanese sailor, Hu Tu Mi, who had escaped from a mental institution in Tampa.

Somehow he made it from Tampa to Lakeland and was now hiding out in the Green swamp. The afternoon the deputies found him, or rather he found them, running out of the swamps he had been hiding in for six months, it took six deputies to wrestle the small man to the ground. The man's capture ended a six month long search for a so-called "wild man" who had been roaming the swamps, killing wild animals and raiding corn fields for food.

Later while in a county jail, Hu Tu Mi related, through an interpreter, that something in the swamp had scared him and caused him to flee from his hiding spot. The interpreter could not translate what Hu Tu Mi had seen. He was asked if it was a bear or panther, which he responded that it wasn't. A couple days later Hu Tu Mi took his own life by hanging himself in the jail cell. To this day, nobody knows what he saw and had scared him so bad. Many believe it could only have been the Skunk Ape.

On 6 June 1976, not far from the Everglades on the southwestern side of Florida in Fort Myers, a watermelon farmer reported seeing a Skunk Ape near his field. John Holley related that he, his brother and a friend were traveling down a dirt road after picking watermelons, at about eight thirty PM, when they saw a large, six foot creature with dark hair covering its body emerge from behind a pine tree and stopped next to the road. Holley stopped his truck and got out. The creature then retreated back into the woods. His brother talked him out of pursuing the animal. Later when Holley brought the sheriff's dept. to the location, they found footprints and dark hair on a barbed wire fence. The sighting was investigated by the Yeti Research Society and the hair samples were sent to the University of Miami for identification. There was no further mention of the hair samples.

Also in June 1976, a Charlotte County deputy sheriff reported seeing a Skunk ape near Grove City, which is located right across the Charlotte Harbor from Fort Myers. Deputy Tom Williams related that he had been dispatched to a sighting by two teenaged boys. When he arrived, he found the boys were terrified and had obviously seen something that troubled them. The boys said they had seen a large hairy creature by a pond next to Roberts Street, an undeveloped area at that time. They then ran to another location and notified the sheriff's office. Deputy Williams then took the boys to their home and returned to the pond alone. He turned on his patrol car lights and saw a large creature, with reddish brown hair covering its body. It was bent over and appeared to be drinking or getting fish from the pond. He reported it was four feet in height in a bent over position. He went on to say he had seen bears, and this creature was unlike anything he'd seen before. With the lights shining on it, the creature got up and walked away back into the nearby woods. Deputy Williams stated that at no time did the creature exhibit any aggressive behavior toward him. He also went on record to say that up until that night, he pretty much thought the sightings were of a bear, but now he believed a large, unknown creature was roaming the swamps.

On 1 January 1976 the *St Petersburg Times* newspaper ran a story about a witness apparently knocked down by a Skunk Ape. John Sohl, an 18 year old student at St Petersburg Junior College, was camping with his six friends at a Rock Crusher quarry near Homosassa Springs. They were sitting around a campfire playing a guitar when they heard something large moving in the woods near them. John decided to go investigate the noise. When John walked up a small hill and looked down into a small valley he observed three hairy beings, one about eight feet in height, one with very definite breasts, and the third about five feet in height. With the stars out, he could make out some but not all of the features of the three creatures. He called out to his friends, one friend arriving in time to see something moving away, but couldn't really tell what it was. John and his friend went back to the truck and got a flashlight and then returned to the sighting location. They didn't find any footprints but did see the broken plants. Not finding anything else, they then returned to their camp.

About half an hour later John went back out to the area, armed with his camera. He found a spot, kneeled down and waited to see if the creatures would return. He didn't have to wait long. John's camera gave off a squealing sound as the flash charged. Apparently one of the creatures heard the squealing and came to see what was making the noise. John stated that he was dressed in a camouflage jacket and didn't think the creature saw him or connected the sound with a human. He heard something behind him and turned with his camera. He saw that the creature was just two feet from him. He snapped a picture and when the flash went off, John found himself being thrown fifteen feet into the air.

He lay on the ground in fear waiting for the creature to return. His friends saw the flash go off and rushed to the location to find John lying on the ground with a look of sheer terror on his face. They immediately searched the nearby area but the creature(s) were nowhere in sight. They then retrieved John's camera and because he had hurt his leg, had to carry him back to the campfire.

Later John had his leg examined at the college clinic but found he was just bruised on his buttocks. The doctor went on to say that it might have been the shock that immobilized John's leg. He also didn't tell the doctor what he had seen. John contacted the Yeti Research Society and related his sighting. Because John had the camera focused on objects thirty feet away, the pictures did not show anything. John only had bruised buttocks to show what happened that night. He told the investigators that he didn't think the creature intentionally hit him, but surprised by the flash, turned around quickly with its long arms and struck John, causing him to go flying back.

During my research, I came across a post on the Bigfoot Encounters site, run by the late Bobbie Short. In the post it related that the sighting was actually a hoax. I contacted John Sohl on Facebook to verify the story and found out that the whole incident was meant as a harmless prank on another student that ballooned and got out of control. The whole hoax story can be found at http://www.bigfootencounters.com/hoaxes/sohl.htm. Mr. Sohl went on to relate that he later contacted the reporter, who wrote the story, and tried to get a retraction on the story but was told "Sorry, old news, No one wants to hear it." Unfortunately, this is one of those many times when the media prefers the fantastic over the truth. Though this story was proven to be a hoax, there are still sightings from that area that haven't been disproven. Mr. Sohl was actually happy and relieved to get the record straight on this event, stating that is was the most embarrassing moment in his life. The story can be found in "The Bigfoot Casebook" by Janet and Colin Bord.

In 2015, I purchased a 1974 Skunk Ape casting that was said to come from an area near Brooksville. I contacted the seller and he related an extraordinary story that went with the casting. The seller asked me not to use his name, but go by John H, due to privacy reasons. John went on to tell that his grandparents purchased a small vacation cabin in 1970 and owned it up until the early 1990's. The cabin was located on the Withlacoochee River in the small town of Nobleton, which is located in Hernando County. His family would visit almost every summer and other holidays. This area had some unusual neighbors, one of which was an albino man in a mobile home downriver. He saw this man swimming in the river, populated with alligators. The local residents referred him as "That crazy albino."

Later John met and got to be good friends with this albino neighbor, who he referred to as "Ed." He later found out Ed was a photographer, had went to Vietnam, and suffered from Post Combat Stress. Ed had moved down to the Florida swamps for solitude. The subject of the Vietnam war was off limits with Ed, preferring to talk about his vegetable garden and another garden. This garden was located on a small island on the river, near his trailer. The small little sub-continent piece of land was called Hog Island, and Ed grew marijuana on it.

John went on to tell that during a time when he was twenty one, he was enjoying a beer with Ed as he went on about it being safe to swim with gators. Ed stopped talking and looked at John and asked him if he had seen or heard of the Coochee Man, which John replied that he hadn't. Ed didn't say another word about it until about a month later, when Ed brought up the topic of the Coochee man again. He went on to say he had picked Hog Island to keep his crop away from prying eyes and that it was uninhabited. Or he had thought it was uninhabited.

With that Ed put down his beer and brought out two large wooden boxes, marked "Off Limits." Ed then went on to tell John that some form of creature like Bigfoot was out on Hog Island. He hadn't actually seen it, but while he was tending his secret garden, he saw flashes of a large dark figure in the distance, but also heard it run away. Ed went on to say that it was extremely fast.

Now John and his family had heard strange loud yells and screams during the night, but always thought they were panthers or drunk hillbillies, but they never saw anything like Bigfoot or the Skunk Ape. When John told Ed about the screams, Ed got excited and told him "You heard the Coochee Man screaming." Ed had named the creature after the Withlacoochee River, where Hog Island was located.

Ed then tapped the wooden box with his fingers and went on to tell John that in 1979, he had gone out to harvest his crop and found half of it destroyed. While looking over the damage, Ed discovered a series of giant footprints made by the unknown culprit. The tracks went off into the swamps. John didn't know what to think but had heard stories about the Skunk Ape. Ed opened the box to reveal two large castings of the giant footprints, one of the left foot and one of the right. John was amazed at the castings, especially at the detail of the footprints. Ed then closed the box and put the boxes back in his trailer and never said another word about it. Ed had moved his secret garden into his trailer and slept on the couch.

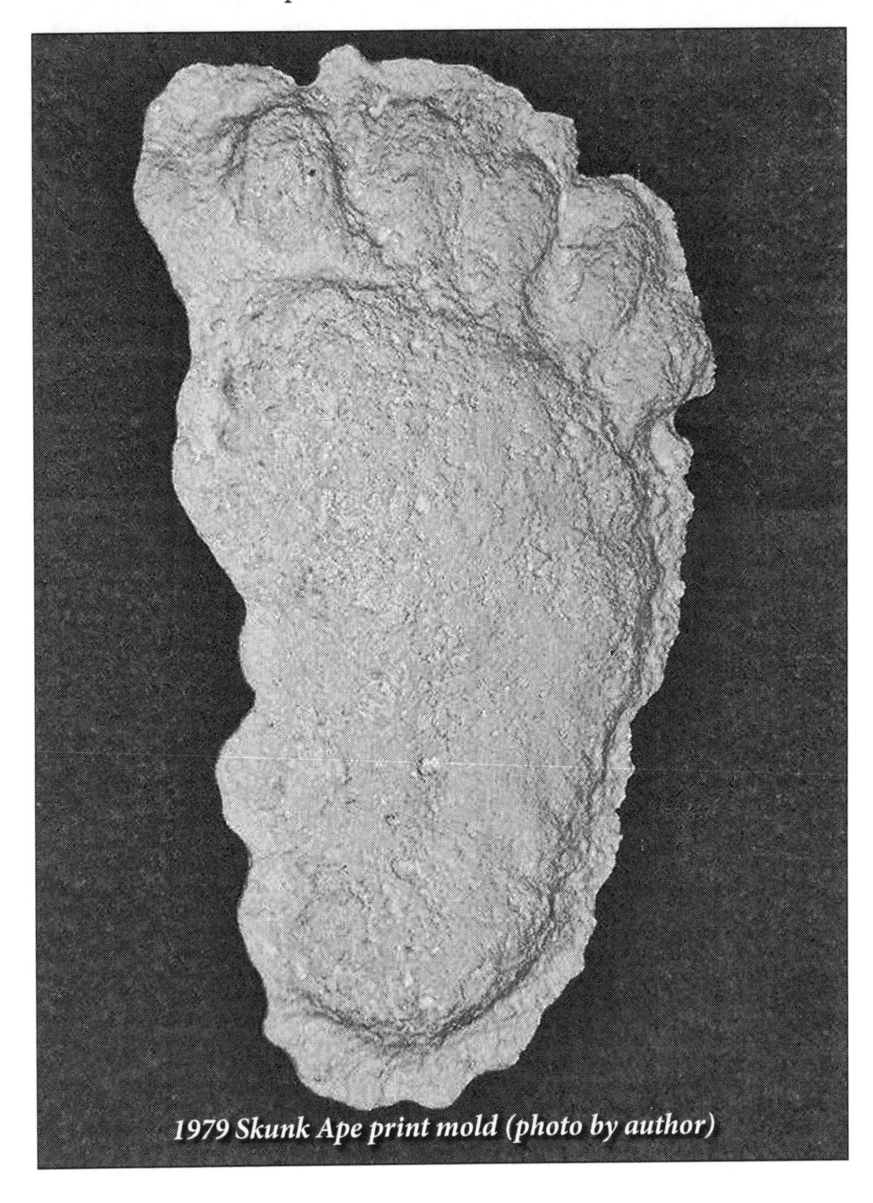

1979 Skunk Ape print mold (photo by author)

To conclude... John's grandparents grew old and ill and had to sell their fishing cabin, he did manage to keep in touch with Ed by phone and even made the drive up there to visit him a few times.

Around October 2015, Ed called John and revealed that he had terminal cancer. Ed related he had no real family or friends, and asked if he could put John in charge of his estate, which John accepted. Ed passed away just a few months later. While cleaning out Ed's trailer, John found the two wooden crates with the plaster Bigfoot/Skunk Ape "Coochee Man" plaster castings. Somehow over the years, the casting of the right footprint broke and now sadly exists in many pieces. John decided to make copies of the left footprint casting and sell it on eBay, which I eventually purchased. I got a hold of John and verified the story and asked if I could use it, which he happily granted me. Today that casting sits proudly next to my copy of the Patterson/Gimlin Bigfoot casting on my wall.

In June 1997 the Skunk ape made the media headlines when a group of British tourists on a tour bus, In Ochopee, Florida, all claimed to have seen a large, hairy ape-like creature walk across the road and then along the banks of the swamp. Later a local fire chief named Vince Doerr managed to snap a photo of the hairy creature as it walked away from him into the swamps in the same area. The picture was widely published in all the Florida newspapers.

Later in Aug of 1997 in Manatee County, three teenage boys say they saw the Skunk Ape in a cemetery in Braden River. This now developed community butts right up to Myakka National Forest. The boys related to police that they went on a night time ghost hunt in the local cemetery, located about half a mile from the trailer court they lived in. Frank Luke, Grant Prince, and Tony Dault left the park just past midnight. As they approached the cemetery, they heard a loud rasping sound which the teens thought was an alligator in pain. There were no other animal sounds and it was deathly quiet. They then proceeded in, stars shining brightly above them. A crashing sound echoed through the night causing them to freeze in their tracks. Grant switched on his flashlight and aimed it towards where the sound originated. Two large, green, glowing eyes stared back at them. The glowing eyes were at least six feet from the ground. This was not an alligator or panther. They quickly fled from the cemetery and didn't stop until they reached the trailer park. They stood there trying to catch their breath and discussed what they had seen. The teens then retreated back into Grant's trailer and played cards. They thought this was the end to their encounter. They were wrong. Something followed them back to their home.

At about 2 am, the living room windows in the trailer were open as the youths played cards, when they detected a foul smell like sewer water. Grant got up and went to the window to see what was causing the odor. As he looked out into the night, a pair of large green eyes were staring back at him. Grant stepped back and yelled to his comrades, who could also see the eyes. The eyes disappeared, but something or someone knocked over a bicycle parked in the yard. They walked outside in time to see a large hairy creature running down Cathy Avenue back toward the cemetery. They were amazed at how fast the animal was, even with it's large hairy arms. They told the police that it ran gorilla style. Slightly bent over as it moved. This story made front page news of the *Sarasota Herald* newspaper with a picture of the boys sitting on the patio of Grant's trailer.

The Skunk Ape has been photographed and filmed numerous times over the last thirty years, but probably the most famous and controversial is the Myakka Skunk Ape photo. In 2000, two photographs and a letter sent by an anonymous woman was mailed to the Sarasota County, Florida, Sheriff's Department. The photographs show what appears to be a large hairy bipedal creature standing next to a large palmetto plant. In the letter, the woman claims to have photographed an ape in her backyard. The woman wrote that on three different nights an ape had entered her backyard to take apples left on her back porch. She was convinced the ape was an escaped orangutan. It should be noted the witness in question at no time called the creature a Skunk Ape, but simply refers to it as an ape believed to have escaped from a zoo. Escaped exotic animals are not uncommon in Florida. During Hurricane Andrew, animals from the Miami Zoo got loose and some were never recovered. Monkeyland, located near Miami, did report losing some spider monkeys during the storms, but none of their larger primates.

As far as the pictures go, the jury is still out on this one. Cryptozoologists believe it to be a real animal, but cannot decide if it is in fact an orangutan or some other unknown primate. Without the witness coming forward and showing exactly where the sightings took place, the photos will continue to remain an unsolved case.

On 8 May 2012, Bigfoot hunter Stacy Brown was out Bigfoot hunting with his dad and friends in Torreya State Park in Northern Florida. They went out equipped with night vision scopes and a FLIR thermal imager. At about midnight the team started hearing something moving around outside their campsite. After hearing some wood knocks, Stacy's dad pointed the FLIR imager in the direction of the knocks. He then spotted something large not far from where they stood. On the imager he saw a large bipedal creature standing behind a tree and appeared to be watching them, then stepped over from behind the tree to another tree. The FLIR picked up the total thermal outline of the creature as it moved. The video is available to watch online and you can see the perfect outline of the creature as it moves.

My wife and I conducted an investigation for ourselves of this sighting and had Stacy take us out to where it happened. I had my wife film me at the same location doing the same movement and compared it to Stacy's. You can plainly see that whatever this animal is, it was a lot larger than me. Unbelievably it is estimated the creature is about eight feet tall. In my opinion Stacy's video stands right up there with the 1967 Roger Patterson film. It is the best evidence to date of the elusive Florida cryptid. The video is available to watch at SasquatchHunters.com.

On an early Thanksgiving morning in 2012, a hunter by the name of Dink Smith was sitting in his hunting stand in the middle of the Green Swamp. He related that he was playing on his cellphone when he caught movement to his left. He glanced up to see at what he first thought was another hunter in a ghillie suit moving out in the large palmetto field in front of him. He noticed that the large being was not carrying a rifle and was moving very gracefully through the palmetto. He knew humans didn't move like that, especially in darkness. He then got a better look at it and realized it was a large creature covered in dark red hair. He stopped his game and switched to the camera on his phone. The creature stopped in the middle of the field and appeared to be sniffing the air. Dink said the creature was about eight feet tall and had a human type face and was extremely muscular.

He aimed his phone and started to film. The creature then suddenly looked up at Dink. He related that a chill shot down his spine as he realized it wasn't a person in a suit, but a real creature. He had heard stories of the skunk ape, but didn't really believe them, until

Robert Robinson with researcher Stacy Brown.
(photo © Legend TripperPhotography)

then. They both stared at each other for what seemed like minutes. He made sure he had his rifle at the ready, but stated that he didn't feel threatened by the creature. Suddenly the creature started running away from him into the nearby swamps. Dink was amazed at how fast the animal ran. After it was out of sight, he sat there and pondered what he had seen. After coming back to his senses, he got on his phone and called his son and father, which were hunting at a different location in the Green swamp. He related what he had seen, and they immediately came out to his location. The son and father noticed that Dink was in a very emotional state and believed what he had seen.

A couple of weeks later when Dink was ready to talk about it, he paid me a visit and told me about what he had seen. The next day, Dink took my wife and I out to the location. We looked over the area where the animal was standing and what direction it went. We did find foot prints but because of the recent rain storms, were unable to make good castings. He showed me the video he took of the creature. But again because of the quality of video and with mist covering the palmetto field, it was difficult to see any compelling details. The video does show a large being standing in the field and then it quickly moves away. I believe that Dink did in fact see something he couldn't explain, and there were fourteen-inch footprints in the mud. My wife took pictures of me, standing where the creature was and compared them with the video. You can see that the creature was about eight foot tall.

Tracking the Skunk Ape (photo by author)

On a side note, the first sighting of the Skunk ape to appear in the newspapers happened in the same Green Swamps in 1947, when a four-year-old boy saw a large hairy bipedal creature standing behind an orange tree, watching him. He quickly went back into his home and related what he saw to his mother. The mother later related that she could still smell the creature, even hours after the sighting.

In March 2013, Mike Falconer and his son were visiting Myakka River State Park in Sarasota County, when he noticed some people on the side of the road pointing to something in the field, next to Lake Myakka. Mike pulled his truck over and stopped. As he got out and looked over to where the people were pointing, he saw a large hairy bipedal creature quickly moving across the large field. He and his son took off running after it. Mike had his cellphone video recording the entire time. While he did manage to capture a large figure crossing the field, it is difficult to determine any distinct features. Cellphones do not offer the best quality for filming and objects appear further out than they really are. The area of Myakka has a long history of Skunk Ape sightings.

Within the soggy expanse of the Everglades sits Skunk Ape Research Headquarters, in the tiny unincorporated community of Ochopee (pronounced oh-CHOP-pee). This small museum/small roadside "zoo" with a gift shop stocked with Skunk Ape memorabilia, is owned and run by Dave Shealy. He has been obsessed with the Skunk Ape since he first spotted one as a boy while hunting in the Everglades. Dave says he has had four sightings and has even filmed the cryptid twice. Dave stated "They're omnivores but can run down a hog and rip it to shreds."

During my research I talked to many airboat ride owners and a lot of them have seen the large hairy cryptid roaming around the swamps. Park rangers on the other hand, assured me that there were no large primates in the Florida swamps or hummocks. They claimed all the sightings were of bears or hunters in ghillie suits.

These large hairy primate creatures, which continue to defy science, still make their presence known in the Sunshine State. Today there is still vast swaths of forest and swampland to offer refuge for this elusive cryptid. As man encroaches more into the last of Florida's forests and swamps, perhaps the day will come when the world will see that these fantastic creatures indeed do exist.

Today there are groups of dedicated researchers who journey into the dark swamps and hummocks on the hunt for the elusive cryptid. The Florida Skunk Ape Project and the Independent Sasquatch Research Team continue this quest. Both have active websites and are always looking for new members.

If you ever decide to visit Florida and venture into the swamps, you just might get to see a large hairy creature prowling through the dark hummocks that we call the Florida Skunk Ape. Keep your eyes - and your mind - wide open.

References

Blackburn, Lyle (2017) Beyond Boggy Creek, Anomalist Books, pp. 226-256. ISBN 978-1-938398-70-4

Coleman, Loren. "Myakka Skunk Ape 'Letter'". The Cryptozoologist. International Cryptozoology Museum.

Coleman, Loren (2001). "The Myakka 'Skunk Ape' Photographs". The Cryptozoologist. International Cryptozoology Museum.

Davis, Phil (1996) In search of the Skunk Ape. XS magazine, Volume 6, No 36 pp. 15-19

Green, John (1978) Sasquatch, Apes Among Us, Cheam Publishing Ltd, pp 270-280, ISBN 0-88839-018-1

Lennon, Vince (2003-10-22). "Is a Skunk Ape Loose in Campbell County?". WATE 6 News. World Now and WATE. Archived from the original on 2007-01-01.

Moore, Jr., Chester (2001-02-22). "X-Files: Alleged 'skunk ape' baffles experts". The Orange Leader. Orange, Texas: Eric Bauer.

Newton, Michael (2005). "Skunk Ape". Encyclopedia of Cryptozoology: A Global Guide to Hidden Animals and Their Pursuers. Jefferson: McFarland & Company, Inc. pp. 430–431. ISBN 978-0-7864-2036-0.

Newton, Michael (2007) Florida's Unexpected Wildlife, University Press of Florida, pp. 73-99, ISBN 978-0-8130-3156-9.

Place, Marian T (1978) Bigfoot All Over the Country, Dodd Mead, pp 167/8, ISBN 978-0396076100

http://www.bigfootencounters.com/hoaxes/sohl.htm

Skunk Ape Research Groups:

The Florida Skunk Ape Project
https://www.floridaskunkapeproject.org/

The Independent Sasquatch Research Team
http://www.isrtusa.com/

Utah High Desert (photo by author)

An Analysis of Relict Hominoid Sightings in the Desert

by Bruce Champagne

For the past few years, a middle-aged housewife living on the edge of the Utah high desert has reportedly watched a large, upright, dark-colored hominoid (Sasquatch) approach and drink from the water trough in her back yard. On more than one occasion, she heard screams and photographed footprints in the soil on her dusty property. Interestingly, this ongoing activity would have required the animal to move exposed over open, sage brush ground for five miles, and adjacent to a relatively busy roadway. I was already familiar with the region and knew the general area had both recent activity and history, and had also located footprints and other reports in the nearby small, Juniper-covered, mountain range.

The temperate rainforests of North America's Pacific Northwest, the forests and wetlands of the southern states, and the Appalachian regions of the northeast have all been identified by researchers as the preferred environments for unclassified relict hominoids. Dr. John Chibnall attempted to provide a contiguous state-to-state correlation between Bigfoot Field Researchers Organization (BFRO) relict hominoid reports and societal characteristics. He reasonably assumed that reports would come from areas with more heavily forested and "gloomy" states, though he eventually found this association was "surprisingly low."

Dr. Chibnall also found that the physical features (relative size, water mass, road miles) of a state were not predictive of reports he analyzed, and ranked states based on the number of reports and the state's human population. Desert states appeared well represented. Utah ranked #10, followed by Colorado (#12), New Mexico (#17), Arizona (#26), California (#29), Texas (#37), and Nevada (#48). With the exception of Nevada, some of these states scored higher than traditionally recognized states for relict hominoid environments.

Colorado Desert (photo: Stuart Fore)

Though desert regions may provide a more challenging, and perhaps less likely, environment for relict hominoids, sightings have always occurred and continue to this day. Among the first relict hominoid sightings in Southern California were of the "Fontana Speedway Monster" of the San Bernardino Mountains, while on the Tule River Indian Reservation, potentially 1000-year-old pictographs of the "Hairy Man" adorn rock walls in Central, California. The "Borrego Sandman" has been reported intermittently from the margins of the Mojave Desert and Death Valley, in Southern California, since 1939. With a similar history, observations of the sandy-colored, "Yucca Man" began in 1971 from the desert areas around Palm Springs, California while the "Mogollon Monster" has been reported in the Grand Canyon and other areas of Arizona. Researchers David Weatherly, JC Johnson, Brenda Harris, and Christopher O'Brien, to name but a few, are well aware of the "Yei Tso," "Crownpoint Howler," and "Arizona Howler" of southwest North America.

But how does a large, unclassified hominoid successfully live in a demanding desert environment? Are the animals actually residing in the desert, or are they merely transiting through when they are observed? I began to consider how a preliminary analysis of relict hominoid reports from desert areas might help evaluate subsequent reports and plan research supporting the eventual scientific description of North American relict hominoids.

The Desert Environment

Desert regions comprise approximately 18% of the earth's land surface and are likely growing in area due to conditions resulting from de-vegetation, over-grazing, and unlimited burning, etc. There may be a perception that the desert is entirely arid with nothing but sand dunes, rock, and cacti to interrupt a bleak, lunar-like landscape. However, the desert is a vibrant and dynamic environment. To be sure, the desert can be demanding and unforgiving, but for a species that can manage to exploit such an expanding and barrier-like (to predators and competitors) environment, an ecological opportunity may await.

There are various descriptions of desert environments, but generically, these regions are identified as receiving less than 10" of average rainfall a year, with high rates of evapotranspiration. As dry as they are, most deserts have some natural water resources resulting from condensation, snow, occasional rains, or from ground water. The soil is alkaline and not only restricts plant growth, but also the individual and population sizes of the animals living there.

Within the North American high deserts, there are multiple sub-climates providing up to 200 biological communities that can be grouped into 6 vegetation zones. The shadscale zone, of the lower valley bottoms and run off areas, creates saline soils. The sagebrush zone of the lower mountain slopes, comprises the largest land area in the desert. At a slightly higher elevation (6000'-8000'), the Pinyon-Juniper community is composed of those trees with a sage underbrush. Montane communities are varied and isolated from other montane communities, as each community may be uniquely impacted by climate and other conditions. Generally found above 10,000' in elevation, the alpine community consists of shorter plants growing above the tree line and continuing downslope in higher latitudes. In these areas, vegetation may also become isolated and unique. Riparian communities may be found in all elevations and zones.

Relict Hominoids in Desert North America

In a preliminary attempt to estimate the distributions of relict hominoids reported in the various desert environments of North America, I reviewed some of the larger databases, assuming that a significant portion of the reports had been vetted. In addition to reports from the BFRO and John Green databases, I added observations from four smaller, regional databases to gather 215 desert area relict hominoid reports from the desert states of Arizona, California, Colorado, New Mexico, Nevada, Texas, and Utah (spanning 1920-2014). I then attempted to position each report, as closely as possible, using the Google Earth satellite photo application, and visually confirmed the observation did occur in one of the desert zones. Where possible, the date and/or season, time, elevation, weather, desert zone type, animals' physical description and behavior(s), and location were recorded and examined.

New Mexico Desert (photo by Stuart Fore)

Nevada Desert (photo: Stuart Fore)

Observed Distributions

The elevations of the locations of the analyzed reports ranged from 180'-12,400', though I noted relict hominoids were more commonly reported from elevations between 7,000'-8,000' (20%), followed closely by 6,000'-7,000' (19%), and 5,000'-6,000' (14%) elevations. Though there were reports from all elevations, reports were minimal for elevations above 8,000' (14% combined).

Distribution through the various desert zones was also varied. Approximately 30% of the reports occurred in the shadescale zone, 24% from the sagebrush zone, 34% from Pinyon-Juniper communities, 10% from montane zones, and 2% from the alpine zone.

Relict hominoids were observed in every season of the year. The summer season accounted for a majority of the reports (mostly in the month of June), at approximately 76%, followed by autumn (30%), winter (19%), and spring (11%). Summer observations appeared to occur more often in the Pinyon-Juniper desert communities, followed by the shadscale and sagebrush zones. Autumn observations occurred in all desert zones, but primarily from the shadscale, sagebrush, and

Pinyon-Juniper communities. Winter reports occurred in most desert zones, and largely in the shadscale and Pinyon-Juniper communities. Springtime observations occurred in each zone, though mostly in shadscale areas.

When a relatively specific time was provided in a report, it was noted the relict hominoids were most frequently observed between the hours of 00:00-03:00 (25%), followed by the periods of 21:00-00:00 (20%), 18:00-21:00 (14%), 15:00-18:00 (11%), 12:00-15:00 (10%), 03:00-06:00 (8%), with the periods of 06:00-09:00 and 09:00-12:00, occurring in 6% of the reports. Observations were reported during all moon phases and weather, and when regarded with temporal distributions, do not appear to be a function of observational effort.

Environmental Descriptions

As I examined the general vicinity of the collected reports, I noted they usually contained relatively small retention ponds, water tanks, hot springs, and irrigation canals, in addition to the natural streams, rivers, lakes, and reservoirs. I understood human habitation and activity could also provide a dependable source of water for a bold or desperate animal and that watering opportunities may also provide for a greater and more predictable concentration of prey species.

Some Native American and other investigators have suggested relict hominoids "follow the river." As could be expected, a significant number of the reports were of animals in close proximity to the known water sources in the area. Approximately 46% of the reports occurred at the water's edge or within 1 mile of the nearest body of water. It was estimated 35% of the reports occurred within a range of 1-5 miles from a dependable water source, 15% from 5-10 miles distant, 5% from 10-20 miles distant, and 3% reported at distances greater than 20 miles from an obvious, dependable water source.

When I investigated the site of the relict hominoid visiting the horse trough, it became apparent how the animal probably travelled from the nearest desert mountain range and across the flat shadscale zone for five miles. It is likely that animal moved through a 30' X 30' ravine that extended from the mountain range to within feet of the water in the horse trough. If the animal did travel this route, it could do so virtually unseen. Interestingly, I observed in 94% of the desert field reports that ravines, gullies, and canyons were typically immediately present, especially when the animal was observed in relative close proximity to human populations. The observations not in association with these geographical features usually included a potential movement corridor of concealing vegetation and/or a river. Other observations in areas with no ravines involved significant resources and opportunities (fruiting crops, remote/isolated water sources) and a low human population density, perhaps reducing any risk of discovery to an exposed animal.

Physical Descriptions

As the desert environment generally influences species towards a smaller size for both individual animals and populations, I was interested if the sizes of relict hominoids would be reflected in that environmental factor. Not all reports provided physical descriptions, and some descriptions were partial.

The height of the majority of the animals was estimated between 6-8' in height (32%). Approximately 9% of the animals were estimated between 8-10' in height, with 8% of the animals reported with a height estimated at less than 6'. Approximately 16% of the reports noted an animal with a heavy or massive physique and 3% of the animals were described with a relatively light build.

When the physical description of observed relict hominoids was reported, there did not appear to be a distinct correspondence between height, build, and hair color or length. There also did not appear to be a regular distinction between the sexes. Smaller animals were reported in multiple observations.

It could be advantageous for a desert animal to have a lighter-colored skin or coat to reflect, rather than absorb, the desert heat and perhaps, provide some type of concealment in the lighter-colored and exposed environment. The majority of the reports described an animal with dark brown hair (16%), followed by light brown hair (13%). Animals were reported with black, red, and gray hair almost evenly (10%). When hair length was reported, the animals were reported with a hair length of 3-6" in 8% of the observations. 5% of the animals were reported with a hair length of < 3".

Animal Activity and Behaviors

Some of the collected relict hominoid observations reported various behaviors, some of which were in association with another behavior. Of the reviewed reports, approximately 22% described the animal(s) making some type of vocalization (screams, whoops, whelps, etc.). 20% of the observations reported a relict hominoid walking on, or crossing a roadway, either bipedally or quadrupedally. Some observations reported the animal(s) watching or approaching the observer(s) in what was perceived as curiosity (15%). Eating and/or drinking was reported in 8% of the observations. Some of the feeding opportunities exploited by the observed animals included drinking from horse troughs, foraging in garbage bins, and entering residences, campsites, vineyards, and orchards. Noted food items included fruit, human food, chickens, rabbits, gophers, and crayfish.

Demonstrated aggression or territoriality (making physical contact with a person, throwing objects, purposeful physical contact with houses and vehicles, etc.) was reported in 7% of the observations. Wood knocks, vegetation/tree destruction, and rock clacks were also attributed to the relict hominoids in 7% of the observations. The animals were observed attempting to conceal themselves in 3% of the observations, and fleeing the area in 2% of the reports. Suspected nests were reported in 1% of the observations.

Discussion and Observations

Using known mammals, and especially primates, as analogs may be helpful in estimating relict hominoid ecology within desert environments. Known as xerocoles, many desert-dwelling animals are specifically adapted to live in these unique and challenging environments. However, some larger mammal species appear capable of exploiting multiple environments- to include the desert. Such mammalian terrestrial megafauna includes cougars *(Felis concolor)*, mule deer *(Odocoileus hemionus)*, pronghorn *(Antilocapra americana)*, and black bear *(Ursus americanus)*. As a result, it would not be inconceivable that relict hominoids may be similarly capable, either as residents or transients in the area.

Of course, *Homo sapiens* have been living in the desert for thousands of years. Other primates, like the Olive Baboon *(Papio anubis),* Vervet Monkey *(Chlorocebus pygerythrus),* Patas Monkey *(Erythrocebus patas),* and two arboreal, nocturnal Galago species are widely distributed throughout the desert environments of Africa.

Olive Baboons live in the widest range of habitats, maintain home ranges of between 2-25 miles^2, travel approximately 1.8-2.5 miles/day foraging, and hydrate every 2 days. Based on pattern analysis, Dr. Jeff Meldrum estimated the relict hominoid home range may be under 18 miles in radius. Though I suspect Dr. Meldrum's home range estimate may be associated with a forest habitat, the sightings in this study are still supportive of Dr. Meldrum's approximation.

Obviously, relict hominoids would have evolved behaviorally and physiologically to be able to successfully exploit desert environments as residents or survive movement through such an ecosystem. Olive Baboons are known to dig wells in the dry river beds of Kenya in search of water. I did collect reports of undescribed hominoids digging in the soil with their feet. Perhaps, they were also attempting a similar behavior to access precious groundwater. Allowably, some of the available water sources would be less-than-optimum, maybe even naturally toxic. The people of the Quebrada Camarones region of Chile's Atacama Desert have evolved an ability to detoxify the naturally-occurring arsenic found in their desert water supply. Perhaps, relict hominoids inhabiting desert climes have a similar capability.

To conserve internal water, baboons are typically less active during the heat of the day. Based on the reported observation times in the desert reports I reviewed, it appears the relict hominoids are probably employing a similar strategy.

Desert Report Distribution (photo by author)

Life sustaining water is a metabolic end product from the oxidation of fats, proteins, and carbohydrates. Carbohydrates may be a scarce commodity in the desert, but the protein sources the relict hominoids have been observed hunting and eating can produce 0.41 grams of water for every gram of protein consumed. Additionally, a gram of fat produces 1.07 grams of water. Conceivably, the diet of the successful hunting and foraging relict hominoid has more flexibility in maintaining distance from a dependable water source.

Conclusion

Desert-dwelling, relict hominoid distributions of gender, age class, body size and type, hair coloration and length, and recognized behaviors do not appear to be significantly different from forest and swamp/wetland environment distributions. Though reported in most desert environments, relict hominoids were most likely to be encountered in the summer months in shadscale, sagebrush, and Pinyon-Juniper areas with an elevation of 5000-8000'. Though they can be encountered at any time of day, relict hominoids appear most active in the desert between the hours of 21:00-03:00. Potentially consistent with the adaptation of known primates, relict hominoids may have become behaviorally flexible to exploit opportunities provided by human habitation and activity. As a result, the animals may maintain a home range in close proximity to human habitation and movement corridors, and possibly within 1-5 miles from a dependable water source. When available, relict hominoids appear to use desert ravines, gullies, and canyons as travel routes and/or avenues of approach.

I noted some reports came from very isolated desert environments, while others were from transition areas between alpine mountain ranges. I originally suspected animals observed in these transition areas may have been migrating through the area to the more hospitable alpine and/or temperate environments when they were observed. Noted researcher John Green found no evidence of relict hominoid migration from the data he had collected, and if Dr. Meldrum's home range estimate is even somewhat applicable to desert environments, and the data collected from this preliminary analysis is objectively reasonable, then actual migration may not be supported, and relict hominoids can indeed, be residents of the desert.

Desert Ravine (photo by author)

Sources

Bigfoot Encounters. http://bigfootencounters.com/.

Bigfoot Field Researchers Organization (BFRO). https://www.bfro.net/GDB/#usa

Chibnall, J. (2017). Physical and Social Characteristics of US States as Predictors of Reports to the Bigfoot Field Researchers Organization (BFRO). *The Relict Hominoid Inquiry* 6:17-32 (2017)

https://en.wikipedia.org/wiki/Great_Basin_Desert

http://voices.nationalgeographic.com/2013/04/09/secret-to-olive-baboon-survival-in-a-barren-desert/ (Retrieved 02/14/2017).

http://www.desertusa.com/desert.html#ixzz4LrMDCkCW (Retrieved 02/14/2017).

Graber-Stiehl, I. (2017). Desert people evolve to drink water poisoned with deadly arsenic. *News & Technology*, Feb. 22.

Green, J. http://www.sasquatchdatabase.com/.

Hocking, K. (2017). The Implications of Primate Behavioral Flexibility for Sustainable Human-Primate Coexistence in Anthropogenic Habitats. *International Journal of Primatology.*

Krantz, G. (1992). *Bigfoot-prints; A Scientific Inquiry into the Reality of Sasquatch.*Johnson Printing Company, Boulder, CO.

Meldrum, J. (2006). *Sasquatch; Legend Meets Science.* Tom Doherty and Associates, LLC, New York, NY.

Nowak, R. and Paradiso, J. (1983). *Walker's Mammals of the World.* 4th edition, John Hopkins University Press, Baltimore, Maryland.

Oregon Bigfoot. http://www.oregonbigfoot.com/database.php.

Pyle, R. (1995). *Where Bigfoot Walks.* New York: HoughtonMifflin Company.

Robbins MM, Ando C, Fawcett KA, Grueter CC, Hedwig D, Iwata Y, et al. (2016).

Behavioral Variation in Gorillas: Evidence of Potential Cultural

Traits. PLoS ONE 11(9): e0160483. doi: 10.1371/journal.pone.0160483.

Southwick, C. (1976). *Ecology and the Quality of our Environment.*D. Van Nostrand Company, New York, NY.

Strain, K. (2012). Mayak Datat: The Hairy Man Pictographs. *The Relict Hominoid Inquiry,*1:1-12.

Weatherly, D. (2016). *Woodknocks; Journal of Sasquatch Research.* Leprechaun Press, Arizona.

http://www.borregospringschamber.com/BorregoHistory/Borrego_Sandman.htm (Retrieved 03/10/2017).

http://www.thepalmspringslocal.com/index.php/6-general/featured/171-the-myth-of-yucca-man
(Retrieved 03/10/2017)

https://sasquatchchronicles.com/the-speedway-monster/
(Retrieved 03/10/2017).

The High Strangeness of Bigfoot

by Joshua Cutchin

Throwing Stones: Class B Reports, Confirmation Bias, & the *Wildnisgeist*

During World War II the American Statistical Research Group (SRG), sought to reduce the number of Allied aircraft downed in combat. Though armor was considered, bulletproofing entire airplanes would render American fighters clumsy and expend excess fuel. To arrive at a practical solution, SRG enlisted several mathematicians, including Abraham Wald.

Being statistically minded, SRG compiled data from pilots whose aircraft safely returned. On average, these planes suffered the most bullet holes per square foot in their fuselage; logically this portion, rather than the fuel system or the engine, benefitted the most from armor without outfitting the entire plane.

Wald, on the other hand, perceived a fundamental flaw in this thinking.

"The armor, said Wald, doesn't go where the bullet holes are," wrote mathematics professor Jordan Ellenberg. "It goes where the bullet holes aren't: on the engines... The reason planes were coming back with fewer hits to the engine is that planes that got hit in the engine weren't coming back."

Wald made a logical inference from an absence of evidence, rather than perceiving the problem from a fixed perspective.

Glass Houses

All anomalists must confess a degree of Bigfoot Envy. Yes, UFOs sometimes produce burn marks in the ground, ghost hunters regularly capture electronic voice phenomenon—but these pale in comparison to the wealth of physical evidence Bigfoot provides.

The phenomenon's existence is supported by alleged hair, tissue samples, scat, and, of course, footprints collected over decades. Even after eliminating hoaxes and misidentification, the sheer volume of evidence eclipses other Fortean disciplines. Such evidence, coupled with the fossil record, strongly suggests we are dealing with *something* physical, likely a relict species of hominoid. That is where a betting man puts his money—a patient betting man, to be sure, but a smart one.

Simultaneously, an abundance of High Strangeness deserves intellectually honest attention (if not reconciliation) from cryptozoologists. Too many staunchly support experiencers of roadside crossings but laugh at witnesses who observe Bigfoot emerging from UFOs or—equally anathema to flesh-and-blood cryptozoologists—perceive telepathic communication during their sightings.

The public at large perceives *all* such talk as delusional; every anomalist and eyewitness, regardless of how "sane" their sighting or research focus, lives in a glass house. Don't throw stones. If a witness' story and character seem reliable, their claims should be examined on their own merit, regardless of one's paradigm.

Try as we might, these phenomena cannot be cordoned into discrete camps. It is incumbent upon the Bigfoot community to engage with the messiness of well documented if improbable events such as the 1973-74 Pennsylvania UFO-Bigfoot flap, or sightings of large, hairy hominoids in "window areas" like Utah's Sherman Ranch and California's Mount Shasta. In these locations, witnesses not only encounter Bigfoot but also UFOs, missing time, ghosts, spirits, mystery lights... even what can only be described as traditional faeries.

If Bigfoot is indeed a relict primate, this is strange company to keep. As researchers, we must entertain the possibility—should these "crazier" stories posses a kernel of truth— these phenomena may be somehow linked.

Class B Reports

On March 13th, 2005, a wife hiking with her husband in Benton County, Oregon, heard a growling sound—" low, deep, like a vibrating growl or snort"—that stopped her in her tracks. After cautiously taking a few steps, the couple saw a baseball-sized rock fly onto the path from a commotion in the brush.

"About 1/4 mile along the trail we hear a loud 'whomp, whomp' like wood against wood sound ahead of us up on the hill," the witness wrote. "My husband describes this sound as a person hitting a tree quite hard with a large log." When the case was reported to the Bigfoot Field Researchers Organization (BFRO), it was deemed a "Class B Report."

The BFRO defines Class B Reports as "where a possible sasquatch was observed at a great distance or in poor lighting conditions and *incidents in any other circumstance that did not afford a clear view of the subject are considered Class B Reports*" [emphasis mine].

In many Class B Reports, witnesses fail to see anything resembling a large, bipedal primate in the forest. They instead report activity suggestive of, but not explicitly attributable to, Bigfoot: tossed rocks, wood knocks, vocalizations, anomalous odors, etc. (While not universal nomenclature within the Bigfoot community, the term "Class B Reports" is used herein to indicate sightings where this behavior—sans Bigfoot—is observed.)

Class B Reports often occur in areas with rich histories of Bigfoot sightings, making it understandable why many cryptozoologists jump to the conclusion Bigfoot is involved. However, given the manner in which unexplained phenomena demonstrably cluster in certain locales, it is hasty to attribute such activity solely to Bigfoot, especially when the creature is not clearly observed—if an unseen assailant throws a rock in the woods, *it simply cannot be conclusively labeled a Bigfoot report.*

To be clear: Bigfoot remains a likely explanation for most Class B Reports. At the same time, intellectual honesty demands we consider other phenomena might be responsible; or, most intriguingly, that there may be a hybrid solution, wherein Bigfoot indeed generate anomalous sounds, odors, and projectiles, albeit in an oblique way.

Like bullet holes in airplanes, we consider what data is *not* present.

Wildnisgeist

The end of 1951 wrecked Anna Duryba. The Ukranian immigrant had invited her fourteen-year-old niece, Kathleen, to winter with her in Chilliwack, British Columbia, only to find her tiny four-room cottage under attack. Something began violently smashing outer walls and breaking windows. Countless visitors and neighbors heard the rappings, sometimes as many as 30 in one evening.

A brief respite in the siege occurred when Duryba, at the urging of her priest, vacated the premises for ten days. The activity, however, picked up right where it left off upon her return.

Sheriff's office employee A.J. Edwards reported:

I have heard the sounds on four occasions. In each case they have come as rapid, violent rappings on the outer wall near a window. All persons in the house were within my range of vision on these occasions, with the exception of Miss Duryba's teen-age niece, who was asleep in her bedroom. Each time I ran outside, but could see no one, although the house was fully floodlit...

On the four occasions when I heard the sounds, they came between 8:00 p.m. and midnight. I am told they have been heard regularly during the day, as well as at night. Windows have been broken on several occasions, including one kitchen window which was broken after it had been protected by a wire screen and sheet of plastic.

The case—"The Chilliwack Poltergeist"—shares similarities with quite a few Class B Reports. Coming from the German *poltern,* "to knock," and *geist,* "spirit," *poltergeists* have been reported for millennia around the world, wreaking havoc in victims' homes.

"In earlier times, reports of poltergeist disturbances cite primarily rock-and dirt-throwing, flying objects, loud noises, strange lights, and other apparitions, terrible smells, rapping, physical and sexual assaults, and shrieks," wrote paranormal investigator and author Rosemary Ellen Guiley. In the modern era, these hauntings include electrical disturbances and, more rarely, physical attacks. Such infestations typically begin and end abruptly, rarely exceeding a few months.

Poltergeists were historically blamed upon demons and spirits of the dead, regularly manifesting during spiritualist séances of the late 19th and early 20th centuries. Beginning in the 1930s, contemporary parapsychologists like Nandor Fodor proposed many cases were actually the result of a living agent, often an adolescent female, whose stress or sexual tension generated psychokinetic activity. This attitude is largely retained in contemporary paranormal circles, and does not necessarily conflict with earlier reports of poltergeist behavior during séances—after all, these ceremonies centered around a single individual as well, typically a female medium. The poltergeist seems tied to individuals, rather than locales.

Since poltergeists are unilaterally reported around agents' homes, it is obvious why few parapsychologists have ever entertained the notion of a wilderness poltergeist—or, to coin a phrase, a *wildnisgeist*. Considering the idea opens up a new realm of possibilities; in many cases, the only thing differentiating poltergeist cases from Class B Reports is their setting. Could the same phenomena—taking place in an outdoor environment, where it is less likely to be labeled as such—explain both poltergeist cases and Class B Reports where Bigfoot is not observed?

The comparison between Bigfoot encounters and poltergeists has been drawn in the past. Fred Beck, survivor of the infamous 1924 "Ape Canyon" attack where multiple Bigfoot allegedly besieged a cabin near Mount St. Helens, Washington, perceived his attackers as spirits, the accompanying thumps on the cabin wall as poltergeist behavior. In later years, cryptozoologists flirted with the connection as well. In a presentation at the 2001 Australian "Myths & Monsters" Conference, Tony Healy reported:

As if the yowie/black panther/bunyip/UFO connection was not weird enough, three cases in our files suggest our Furry Friends might also have something in common with poltergeists.

For example, in 1946, when George Nott and his family moved into a long-abandoned property near Wilcannia, they heard thumping sounds in the ceiling. Doors swung open, objects flew, and so many pebbles fell on the roof that they "sounded like a heavy shower of rain." At the same time as this classic poltergeist phenomena, huge human-like tracks appeared in the yard and a large, very irate hairy ape-man began to invade the house, once trying to drag Mrs. Nott outside.

Other researchers brave enough to broach the subject include Greg Newkirk, Dana Matthews, Linda Godfrey, and Loren Coleman.

"Rock-tossing poltergeists are frequently reported in the archives to be found in many kinds of non-cryptozoological studies," Coleman wrote in 2008. "Should old and new accounts of stone-throwing poltergeists be re-evaluated as possible evidence of Bigfoot activity, or should unseen 'Sasquatch' or 'Windigo' said to be throwing rocks be re-evaluated as poltergeists?"

To reiterate: none of this suggests Bigfoot do not exist, nor that they are not responsible for many Class B Reports. Rather, the implication is that we may simply ascribe more activity to them than they deserve. While similarities between poltergeist phenomena and Bigfoot have been noted in passing, few have carefully examined their depth, and even fewer seriously entertained the *wildnisgeist* concept.

Generalities

English researchers Alan Gauld and A.D. Cornell were the first to conduct a large-scale analysis of poltergeist infestations in the late 1970s. After examining 500 international cases from 1800, they found 63 points of commonality, including:

64% of cases featured the manipulation of small objects, including movement, disappearances, and *apports,* or spontaneous transference from one location to another;

- 58% peaked after nightfall;
- 48% involved rapping sounds;
- 36% included the movement of heavy furniture;
- 24% exceeded 365 days;
- 16% featured communication between poltergeist and apparent agent;
- 12% involved opening/closing doors/windows.

Gauld and Cornell also determined, in cases where the activity centered on a human agent, they were most likely female and less than 20 years old. (It is worth noting the propensity for poltergeists to focus on an *individual,* rather than a location, might explain the problems inherent in repeat witnesses, who seem to have all the luck encountering Bigfoot activity while other researchers go their entire lives empty handed—perhaps the behavior they observe is generated by themselves, rather than an exterior source.)

A few points of comparison between poltergeist and Bigfoot experiences immediately emerge from Gauld and Cornell's study. For example, while no shortage of daytime encounters exist, many Bigfoot reports—Class B and otherwise—occur nocturnally.

"According to John Green's database, about 60% of sightings happen during the day," Cliff Barackman wrote. "Just for simplicity, let's say that it's 50/50... Let's also assume that there are maybe 10% as many people out at night as during the day, and those people can see perhaps 10% as far/much. Those simple numbers indicate that bigfoots are probably 100 times more active at night!"

Typical poltergeist agents are young and female, a data point resonant with Bigfoot lore. Legends universally describe the creature's keen interest in young women and children, even abducting them as in the (possibly apocryphal) case of 17-year-old Serephine Long. This attraction to both youth and women remains a minor meme in the Bigfoot community: during the 2000 collection of the celebrated Skookum cast, investigators broadcast recordings of children playing and infants crying to attract Bigfoot, while other researchers employ used feminine products hung from trees as bait, convinced female pheromones attract the creatures.

Poltergeists attach to female youths; youth and females attract Bigfoot.

Throwing Stones

A harrowing account from Linda Godfrey described a 1967 encounter on the Illinois Des Plaines River. The witness heard a peculiar bird call from the opposite bank, drawing his attention to a tall, hairy figure emerging from the forest. The beast was dipping its hands into the shallows, gathering water and searching for food. After the witness failed to stifle a cough, he ducked into the brush and watched in terror as the Bigfoot began wading across the river. From his hiding place, he saw the creature pluck several large, flat stones from the riverbed and toss them exactly where he had been standing moments earlier, hoping to flush him out.

Though its conclusion undermines a flesh-and-blood interpretation of the creature—it literally vanished after the witness yelled, "Oh Jesus, help me, help! Help!"—this story clearly indicates Bigfoot, whatever they may be, throw rocks.

Among known animals primates, especially chimpanzees, are the only ones that exhibit stone-throwing prowess. In Bigfoot sightings, this behavior is consistent throughout the historical record: Dr. John Bindernagel found reports of rock throwing dating back to 1846. An 1877 newspaper article from Bennington, Pennsylvania mentioned a fat, hairy "wild man" with an affinity for "throwing stones at barns." 115 years later, a light-brown, hairy, man-sized creature was observed tossing rocks at a National Park maintenance man driving through Northern California.

At the same time—to use an old adage—all fish swim, but not everything that swims is a fish. While Bigfoot throw stones, it is possible not every stone thrown comes from Bigfoot.

Class B Reports regularly describe stones tossed by invisible assailants. In 2005 a Virginia policeman heard a loud vocalization from a distant ridge while camping. Once his comrades fell asleep, he began to notice repetitive clicking sounds; though they were coming from pebbles bouncing off a nearby picnic table, he saw no one throwing them. The following morning he distinctly heard "Russian or Eastern European and an Asian language of some kind" drifting from the woods.

Rocks striking homes are attributed to Bigfoot without a second thought to poltergeists. An elderly Florida couple reported an eerie cry and foul odor near their property in 2013, culminating in multiple stones hitting their home and outdoor furniture. Despite Bigfoot's absence, the report nonetheless found its way to BFRO.

As noted, incorporeally tossed objects, especially stones, usually indicate a poltergeist infestation. Beginning in 1965, a family in Jaboticabal, Brazil endured a rain of bricks inside their home, followed by a shower of stones—312 in total. In such cases, the stones are usually "warm to the touch." The famous 1998 Humpty Doo poltergeist of Australia produced rocks "not just warm, but very hot" when held by witnesses. Some contend this is because objects traversing other dimensions gather heat.

During 1978's Minerva, Ohio Bigfoot sightings, the Cayton family repeatedly had stones thrown at their roof from the ridgeline behind their home by an unseen assailant. Roofs, it should be noted, are prime targets for poltergeists: in late 1921, stones began striking warehouses in Chico, California, culminating in a March 9, 1922 shower of "rocks ranging in size from peas to baseballs" on the roof of a building owned by J.W. Charge.

The Minerva stones also featured another connection to poltergeist activity.

"One night we were curious to see what would happen... [before] we'd throw a rock up there, we'd mark it with a big 'X' with a marker," said Howe Cayton, a boy at the time. " We'd throw it up on the strip mine—couple minutes later that same rock would come back down with the marking still on it, and the rock would be warm... It was weird how that rock would come back down to us that we'd marked, and have the exact same markings there."

Rapping & Prints

Raps are a hallmark of poltergeists. In the 1661 Drummer of Tedworth case, the Mompesson family was plagued for weeks not only by drumbeats but also raps, apports, disembodied voices, apparitions, and foul smells. In the 19th century, the Epworth Rectory poltergeist wracked an English home with raps and knocks so hard they shook the very walls. Raps are commonly interpreted as spirit communication during séances—in fact, such activity at the Hydesville, New York home of the Fox Sisters birthed the entire spiritualist movement.

It takes little imagination to draw comparisons between wood knocks—sounds of wood-on-wood in the forest, speculated to be Bigfoot communication of some kind—and the rappings of poltergeists. A more direct comparison can be made when Bigfoot are accused of assaulting witnesses' homes with knocks and slaps. In the aforementioned Minerva Monster case, for example, the Caytons reported regular pounding and taps on their outside walls and windows.

This interference extends to rooftops. In 1973, a Monogahela, Pennsylvania family reported sulfurous odors, shadowy apparitions, and odd screams in the area around their home. On the evening of August 24, they distinctly heard "something heavy walking on the roof"—as this was during the area's infamous Bigfoot-UFO flap, the commotion was attributed to Bigfoot.

After making several wood knocks in October 2008, a Bigfoot enthusiast near Little Switzerland, North Carolina received responses from the forest and, later that evening, "was startled awake by what sounded like heavy foot thumping on the roof... I heard another couple of thumps that sounded as if they came from the area over the closet." Later, the raps grew so loud the witness was convinced someone—or something—was trying to break in.

Even beyond showers of stones, similar rooftop thumps are not uncommon in poltergeist cases. The 1878 poltergeist of Amherst, Nova Scotia centered around 19-year-old Esther Teed, whose presence generated rapping sounds as if someone were slamming the roof with a sledgehammer; no culprit was ever observed.

Critics will counter Bigfoot, unlike poltergeists, leave behind clear trace evidence of their domestic attacks. In 1962, for example, a muddy 11-inch handprint was left on the side of a home slapped in Fort Bragg, California. To be pedantic, there is no proof Bigfoot left that print—beyond that argument, poltergeist infestations can also generate anomalous footprints. In 1956 London's Battersea Poltergeist left a single, large footprint in white powder spilled across the floor —the lack of a path in or out of the powder brings to mind how lines of some suspected Bigfoot tracks abruptly end in the middle of empty fields.

Disembodied Voices

In the mid-1970s, Bigfoot researchers Ron Morehead and Alan Berry recorded a series of peculiar vocalizations in California's Sierra Nevada Mountains after leaving a microphone on a branch near their cabin. Morehead's recordings, dubbed the "Sierra Sounds," seem to feature multiple individuals grunting, snuffling, incomprehensively conversing, even bickering; a retired United States Navy crypto-linguist contends they represent an unknown language spoken by nonhuman entities.

As evidenced in the 2005 Virginia report, similar vocalizations are heard throughout North America. The gruff, vaguely Asiatic speech pattern of the Sierra Sounds—colloquially referred to as "Samurai chatter" —has fueled speculation ever since their release: are anomalous voices in the forest, particularly those speaking an unintelligible language, evidence of Bigfoot?

"[They] do not sound like ordinary human voices; at least not to begin with," wrote paranormalist Colin Wilson. "[They] begin in a guttural voice that sounds as if it is made up from grunts and groans."

Though Wilson could easily be describing Morehead's Sierra Sounds, he was actually writing about the manner in which voices evolve in poltergeist infestations.

Disembodied voices are a hallmark of poltergeist infestation. In the 19th century, Ballechin House of Perthshire, Scotland suffered from a variety of poltergeist phenomena, including, knocks, raps, odd odors, the sound of explosions, and (like the voices Sierra Sounds) "the sound of people quarreling." Similar vocalizations were heard in the Drummer of Tedworth case. In one of the most famous modern reports, a disembodied voice calling itself Gef—claiming to be a mongoose—took up residence in an Isle of Man home in 1931, chatting at length with the family and lending an unseen hand to household duties. While on its face absurd, parapsychologists widely regard the case as a deceptive poltergeist manifestation, rather than a talking animal.

Class B witnesses report a variety of auditory evidence. Vocalizations shared between poltergeists and Bigfoot include:

- Heavy breathing. It is not uncommon for Class B Reports to include the sound of heavy breathing, often noted after witnesses retire to their tent or sleeping bag. Similar sounds were heard at Ballechin House and in many other poltergeist cases: "I could distinctly hear and feel something breathing on me."
- Whistles. Whistles in the night are often attributed to

Bigfoot. One Native American witness from Port Hudson, Washington, remembered call-and-response sessions in her youth with whistling Bigfoot at dusk ("You come in right now and quit whistling with Seeat-kos!" her mother chided). Poltergeist cases such as the 17th century Devil of Glenluce, Scotland were known not only for anomalous voices, but "shrill whistles" as well.

- Heavy movement and laughter. In 1875 France's Calvados Castle suffered from poltergeist activity including shrieks, disembodied voices, and sounds of galloping, stampeding, and laughter. Class B Reports often include the sound of heavy movement through the forest, presumably created by a lumbering Bigfoot. Laughter also appears: in a 2005 BFRO report, a Washington camper heard what could only be described as "three or four bizarre shrieks of some sort, a little higher, which almost sounded like some kind of goofy laughter."
- Animal noises. Hairy hominoids worldwide are attributed powerful mimicry abilities. A Chinese farmer observed a wild man in 1977 that "uttered 11 or 12 different sounds… a sparrow chirping, dog barking, pony neighing, leopard growling, and an infant crying." In North America, Bigfoot is ascribed similar skills. In comparison, the sounds heard most often in poltergeist cases include human cries, animalistic growls and snarls, and even—in the Epworthy Rectory incident—turkey gobbles.

Odors & Animal Reactions

While the various odors noticed in anomalous encounters—particularly those present in spirit phenomena, UFOs, and Bigfoot reports—are detailed at length in my book *The Brimstone Deceit* , the topic is worth repeating here. Foul smells, often compared to hydrogen sulfide (rotten eggs, feces, decay, etc.) are common to both Bigfoot and poltergeist reports.

Joseph Glanvill, witness to the Drummer of Tedworth case, claimed the spirit "left a sulphurous smell behind it, which was very offensive." The 1974 poltergeist of Bridgeport, Connecticut generated an odor compared to burning matches and sulfur. In a more modern example, an Englishwoman allegedly cursed by a Bantu shaman returned from South Africa to find her home afflicted by a poltergeist which produced "an unpleasant smell, as of a rotting corpse… sulphur."

Any cryptozoologist will recognize similar odors in Bigfoot literature. The stench of hydrogen sulfide (commonly conflated with sulfur) appears alongside smells of skunk, musk, wet dog, decay, and body odor both in clear sightings and Class B Reports alike. In 1975, a witness and friend noticed "a rotten egg sulphur smell that was over powering [sic]" while trapping near Waupun, Wisconsin; despite no other Bigfoot activity, it was reported to the BFRO. In another case from 1976, a California witness noticed large footprints outside his cabin accompanied by a smell like a wet dog crossed with rotten eggs.

The witness's attention was drawn outside because his family's horses were "going nuts and running in circles." Domestic animals exhibit such behavior regularly in Class B Reports.

"Despite the fact most large breeds of dogs are not afraid of any wildlife known to be native to North America, there is no doubt that something in the North Carolina Smoky Mountains terrorizes them and sends them into an uncharacteristic panic," wrote investigators Tom Burnette and Rob Riggs. Indeed, so-called habituators—those who allege Bigfoot inhabit their property—often possess only circumstantial evidence for their claims; not only the raps, vocalizations, prints, and odors already mentioned, but fearful pets as well.

In May 2010, the dog of an Illinois witness ran back to its owner "with the hair all the way up from her neck and all the way down to her tail, and her tail all the way between her legs and her head down." According to the report, the dog—which disappeared into the brush after several grunts and an odor of decay was noted—had never behaved in such a manner. Shortly thereafter, the owner discovered large footprints alongside a nearby creek.

Animals react identically in other anomalous encounters—including poltergeist cases. The Epworth Rectory Poltergeist so troubled the reverend's manservant that he took the family mastiff to his room; the first evening in his care, the dog barked violently before the noises began, only to whimper and flee on each subsequent evening. Similarly, watchdogs at Calvados Castle turned to whimpering messes when brought in to scare off potential intruders.

In *The Brimstone Deceit,* I suggest pets, with their delicate sense of smell, might react to subtle odors emitted by all unknown phenomena, hence their heightened anxieties in such circumstances. Perhaps, contrary to so much speculation, animals cannot see things invisible to humans, but can rather *smell them.*

Apports & Disapports

In 2011, a Boy Scout leader and his friend caught a vague glimpse of a tall figure wading through a creek near Boone, North Carolina. After spending a restless evening in his car surrounded by strange pops, cracks, and movement in the forest, the witness arose to fetch breakfast.

"The bear hang had been taken down, but not ripped down," the witness said. "It had been untied and dropped down. The bag was open, and all the fresh produce was gone." The dexterity involved suggests human theft; the fact canned goods were left behind implies otherwise.

Though bears and raccoons are most likely to blame for food stolen in the outdoors, some activity brings this assumption into question. Witnesses report adroit thefts from inaccessible bear hangs, zipped backpacks, even latched outbuildings. Besides food, other objects taken include beads, balls, toys, and trinkets, particularly during "gifting" scenarios.

Commonly practiced among habituators, gifting involves leaving objects outside in the hope of attracting Bigfoot activity. Though mundane wildlife activity may be responsible when gifts like food are taken outright, this likelihood is rendered impossible when items are left in exchange. In one particularly compelling example, habituators on a Washington property—regularly troubled by thrown stones, wood knocks, and suspicious cairns appearing overnight—left a large bag of apples hanging from a tree in 2011. The following morning several apples were taken and, in their place, ten dead field mice were found woven in blades of grass. Suffice to say, this behavior is not attributable to bears or raccoons.

Such activity not only shares strong similarities with Celtic faerie belief (wherein offerings would be left out for helpful spirits), but is also a chief feature in both poltergeist cases and séances. In parapsychology circles, objects that seemingly appear out of thin air are known as *apports.* Every alleged Bigfoot gift has precedent in the psychic literature as an apport: food, fruits, stones, even dead rodents, once produced by 19th century medium Eusapia Palladino.

The reverse side of the coin—and even more common among poltergeists— are missing items, sometimes called *disapports.* Each case seems to have its own preferred object: Australia's 1957 Dickson Poltergeist interfered with pencils, England's Borley Rectory Poltergeist stole boots and dictionaries in the 19th century, and in the late 1960s "Fred," the poltergeist of Pontefract, England, was fond of removing eggs from the kitchen only to smash them in the living room.

These disturbances can be quite violent.

"The more vindictive poltergeist can make your house look like it's been ransacked," wrote paranormal author Debi Chestnut. This ability for poltergeists to wreak havoc in victims' homes is sporadically reflected in Bigfoot cases. In the alleged Snelgrove Lake Incident of 2002, almost everything was torn from the walls of an Ontario cabin, including the bathroom sink and refrigerator; bear were ruled out due to the time of year and lack of claw marks (critics of the poltergeist connection will astutely counter that not only was a bloody footprint collected at that site, but poltergeist rarely act in empty houses—the case is presented simply for its thematic relevance).

Electrical Interference & Anomalous Lights

While other aspects of Class B Reports can be chalked up to unseen flesh-and-blood Bigfoot lobbing stones, wood knocking, and vocalizing, it is much more difficult—nigh impossible—to attribute electrical interference to a relict hominoid, yet field researchers nonetheless experience such difficulties.

Such effects are simply expected in poltergeist reports. Researchers investigating a poltergeist infestation in Keene, New Hampshire recorded "abnormally rapid battery drainage," an effect noted by ghost hunters in a variety of purportedly haunted locales. Other electrical interference is more dramatic; in one case from 1990s Glasgow, a poltergeist sufferer regularly had lights switch themselves on and off in his flat, in addition to the failure of two refrigerators, five or six vacuums, six stereos, eight televisions, and countless light bulbs.

"Ghost hunters have long lamented the strange ability of spirits to kill electronic equipment, whether it be draining fresh batteries in a matter of minutes, causing camera malfunctions during critical moments, or even straight up frying electronics," Greg Newkirk wrote. "Turns out, this is something many Bigfoot hunters have experienced as well. In fact, back in 1993, the Bigfoot Research Project, the first serious attempt to capture Sasquatch on trail cameras, made use of a direct video feed fed into an off-site VHS recorder, and was plagued by mysterious problems with its electronic gear, causing numerous issues when it came to capturing evidence."

In fact, such malfunctions are more common in Bigfoot sightings than one might expect. According to one set of researchers, a Leyden jar—a rudimentary capacitor—was fully charged and taken to an area known for Bigfoot habituation, but "within a matter of minutes, the thing had been completely discharged." Ron Morehead, producer of the Sierra Sounds, noticed similar difficulties with his recording equipment:

We had our cameras... all something going wrong with them, our batteries would go dead up there [in the Sierras], Scott Nelson, the crypto-linguist that rode up there, he would have his batteries failing, he went up there with enough batteries to last forever, but also they wouldn't work... My batteries, my brand-new lithium batteries... This was in 2011. I was by myself, when I heard this big pop right outside my tent... I really think it might've not been something hitting a tree, like I originally thought, but maybe something energetically coming out of the tree...when I heard the chatter later, I tried to turn my recorder on, and the batteries were dead. Brand new lithium batteries. I just put them in when I got there, I checked them and everything was fine, they wouldn't work later.

Even more confounding are examples where anomalous orbs of light are recorded in sites of heavy Bigfoot activity. As with reports of electronic interference, most cryptozoologists only open up about such peculiarities in confidence, but the trend remains strong, and is becoming more visible in the Bigfoot community.

"Ghost lights" are regularly seen on Bragg Road in East Texas's Big Thicket, an area famous for Bigfoot sightings. One group of visitors to the area were "dramatically converted" by such a sighting. From Burnette and Riggs:

Like many serious Bigfoot investigators, they thought such

accounts detract of unknown hominid sightings—that introducing things like ghost lights could reduce Bigfoot to the realm of the paranormal... Without their saying so, I was sure they never expected to see any mysterious lights.

We drove about two or three miles up the Ghost Road from the south end. About fifteen minutes later, we were all surprised to see a half dozen or so lights moving about and blinking in the tree branches fifteen or twenty feet off the ground just behind us and to our right as we faced northward... Eight of us were there, and we all saw the lights. They were about the size of golf balls, however, compared to only one basketball-size light in the more typical ghost light sighting. They remained in the tree branches and did not hover over the roadbed to allow us a better look. After several minutes of almost seeming to play hide-and-seek with us, the lights simply vanished.

Correlations, as it is famously said, *do not* mean causation—but they do imply a link. In February 2016 Wes Germer, host of the popular *Sasquatch Chronicles* podcast, and his brother revisited the area of their 2012 sighting, only to observe strange balls of light flying around" the woods near Yacolt.

"We were up on a ridge line watching it for a long time," he wrote. "We decided to go down to where the lights were and found nothing. Upon returning to the ridge line there was not one ball of light but three."

Anomalous lights are part and parcel for ghost activity, including poltergeist cases. Strange lights were seen in Borley Rectory, witnesses saw "glimmering lights that appeared in the children's bedroom" in the Drummer of Tedworth case, etc.

As with other signs of poltergeist activity, mediums and séances generate anomalous light phenomena as well. British medium Stella Cranshaw was surrounded by poltergeist phenomena into her 20s, including the movement of small objects, rappings, and flashes of light. At a methodical series of séances in Norfolk, England in the 1990s—known as The Scole Experiment—researcher Montague Keen recorded lights that would "dart around at great speed and perform elaborately patterned dances in front of us, including perfect, sustained circles executed at high velocity and with a precision which appeared inconsistent with manual manipulation."

Thrown stones, raps, disembodied voices, anomalous odors, frightened pets, apports, electric interference and anomalous lights—we are left with a compelling list of similarities, but it is unclear exactly what, if anything, they mean. Before bridging that gap, let us first examine several substantial counterarguments.

Counterarguments

Considering the alternative concept of the wildnisgeist renders one vulnerable to charges of "cherry picking" by critics, who might argue such cases are only selected because they fit the hypothesis. It is true the above Class B Reports are selected because they fit specific criteria; however, they represent but a small number of a large subset of alleged Bigfoot cases, and as such deserve scrutiny removed from the baggage of the Bigfoot community. Further, the intention is not to work backwards from an alternative idea, but rather to propose a means of combating confirmation bias and keeping assumptions in check; to not answer one unknown with another unknown, but to rather open up another path of inquiry when investigating anomalous activity in the wilderness. In this sense we are not cherry-picking, but instead attempting to view Class B Reports from a different perspective.

We are looking for where the bullet holes aren't.

A major flaw in the wildnisgeist idea is the absence of spontaneous fires, a major signifier of poltergeist activity, in Class B Reports. For example, the Amherst Poltergeist frequently combusted old newspapers, and the Borley Rectory Poltergeist may have actually burned the building down —if any comparable precedent exists in Bigfoot literature, it is highly underreported (in fact, some legends refer to Bigfoot as "Indians Without Fire"). While areas with high numbers of sightings are occasionally ravaged by wildfire, it is specious to assume Bigfoot starts them when plenty of rational explanations exist.

Another stumbling block is a lack of anomalous writing. Poltergeist cases often, but not always, feature writing from unknown sources on walls and mirrors in a variety of media, from lipstick to charcoal and ink. Like anomalous fires, no apparent analogue exists Class B Reports without drawing extremely tenuous connections to stick structures as some form of primitive communication.

Perhaps the most damning counter to the wildnisgeist concept is that, outside Class B Reports, Bigfoot *are* witnessed engaging in much of the above activity (tossing rocks, vocalizing, etc.). Certainly bringing in a wilderness poltergeist violates Occam's Razor, i.e. multiplying variables unnecessarily. It is far more parsimonious to simply assume Class B Reports are due to Bigfoot.

But what if large, hairy creatures are themselves physical manifestations of wildnisgeists?

Hairy Poltergeists

In late November 2002, Indiana resident Greg Yost was fresh off losing his welding job and taking some time to clear his head near the Hoosier National Forest with his dog. The last thing he expected was an encounter with what he deemed Bigfoot.

"All of a sudden up on this big hill, I started hearing this loud crashing noise," Yost said. "Trees branching, branches breaking… About 20 feet up the hill, it stopped… Then I hear him breathing… I could almost feel the vibration from him breathing." Yost escaped with his dog, but, realizing he had left his cooler behind, returned immediately and managed to glimpse "what looked like a left hand and a forearm. It had big old black fingers that looked like cigars, and the fingernails were black… It had hair on him, the hair was hanging off, and it got hairier as it went up his forearm."

Since then, he claims to have had contact with Bigfoot on several other occasions, including observing the creatures in greater detail. Most strikingly, Yost feels he has recorded Bigfoot in a forest saying—in a British accent, no less—"Yaywah, what is that?" followed by wood knocks and Samurai chatter. According to Yost, this audio appeared on a different section of the tape than had been recording.

Regardless of what one suspects of his credibility or mental health, the similarities between Yost's experiences and poltergeist phenomena are confronting. His encounters are witness-centered, rather than location-specific; began during a stressful *liminal* time in his life, when he was between jobs; began with an unseen assailant throwing stones, making loud noises, and breathing heavily; and later involved peculiar voices and the manipulation of objects.

The natural riposte, as noted, is to point out that Yost saw a hairy arm in his initial experience, and has since seen what can only be described as Bigfoot in subsequent encounters. However, the appearance of hairy limbs—or even full apparitions of hairy creatures—has been noted in poltergeist cases, hauntings, and séances.

To cite a handful of examples:

- In 2001 in KwaZulu-Natal, South Africa, a family of five claimed to have been terrorized by a poltergeist which growled, rang telephones, spoke in multiple languages, lobbed produce at anyone inside the home, and smeared lotions and detergents on the walls. According to the youngest son, aged 10, the poltergeist appeared as "hairy and ape-like with sharp nails."
- During the Battersea Poltergeist case, the couple's daughter—15-year-old Shirley—experienced the sensation of something hairy in her bed one evening. When her father looked, the sheet and mattress were ripped to shreds.
- During his 1902 Parisian séances, medium Auguste Politi levitated a table, produced anomalous lights, and touched sitters with a hairy hand—all while bound at the neck, wrists, and feet.

In his book *Wildman: The Monstrous and Mysterious Saga of the British Bigfoot,* author Nick Redfern uncovered perhaps the most striking example of a hairy hominoid observed in conjunction with poltergeist activity. In the 1950s, paranormal author Stan Gooch saw a prehistoric man materialize during a séance in Coventry, England, before vanishing into thin air.

This was a crouching ape-like shape, which became clearer as the moments passed. I guess it approximated to most people's idea of what an ancient cave man would look like. Yet one could not make out too much detail—the eyes were hidden, for example. It stood in half shadow, watching us, breathing heavily as if nervous. I must say, though, that I sensed rather than heard the breathing. I could not decide whether our visitor was wearing the skin of some animal, or whether it had a rough coat of hair of its own.

Famed medium Franek Kluski also allegedly materialized a "mysterious ape" during the early 20th century, and Redfern also investigated a 1985 case where a Bigfoot appeared following an Ouija board session in Rochester, New York. (As an aside, it should be noted that poltergeist activity was sometimes attributed in English folklore to *boggarts,* hirsute faerie folk... further reinforcing the under-appreciated similarities between older traditions and modern Bigfoot reports).

Since the precedent exists, it stands to reason—however unlikely—some Class B Reports wherein a hairy form is glimpsed may fit the wildnisgeist parameters as well.

Wildnisgeist: A Series of Hypotheses

Despite so many similarities between poltergeists and Class B Bigfoot Reports, it is quite unclear what connection exists between the two, if any; the wildnisgeist theory is flawed, at best. Even so, a handful of possibilities seem apparent.

1. There is no Bigfoot or wildnisgeist involved in Class B Reports. In this scenario, all activity described where no assailant is seen—stone throwing, rapping, disembodied voices, odors, etc.—are entirely coincidental and can be written off in these cases as natural phenomena. Showers of stones might be dropped from birds, wood knocks might simply be breaking limbs or woodpeckers, odors might be unseen rotting carcasses... and all might be simple misidentification.

2. Bigfoot and wildnisgeist just happen to exist in the same locations. Here we have multiple sub-scenarios at play. There might be a wildnisgeist attached to an area inhabited by Bigfoot, or a witness finds him/herself in an area known for Bigfoot sightings and generates their own poltergeist activity. If true, it implies Class B Reports come from *both* wildnisgeist and Bigfoot. In any case, this hypothesis is predicated on a complete and utter coincidence between clear Bigfoot sightings and Class B Reports, which remains unlikely.

3. Bigfoot is solely responsible for Class B Reports. Most cryptozoologists endorse this hypothesis. It is undoubtedly the simplest explanation, arguably the most logical. This explanation is not without serious shortcomings, however—specifically the electrical interference and anomalous lights seen in some reports—unless one fully engages with

more taboo theories like Bigfoot as ghosts, spirits, or inter-dimensional creatures, problematic concepts in their own right.

4. Wildnisgeists are responsible for all Bigfoot reports. We jump from the least controversial hypothesis to the most. In this scenario, the wildnisgeist is either attached to a location—explaining areas of plentiful Bigfoot sightings—or, in traditional poltergeist fashion, the witness brings the phenomenon with them as an agent. In either case, sightings of large, hairy hominoids are not flesh-and-blood primates, but instead projected representations of wildnisgeists, nonphysical in nature but possessed of the ability to interact with the physical world as any poltergeist can.
5. Wildnisgeists are poltergeists generated by Bigfoot. Rosemary Ellen Guiley wrote poltergeists seem to be the product of "destructive juvenile or unbalanced adult minds." Plenty of sightings describe Bigfoot acting erratically or angrily, as well as displaying a playful disposition or childish behavior—is it possible flesh-and-blood primates generate poltergeist activity, similar to unstable human beings? As noted, poltergeist cases commonly involve spontaneous fires and anomalous writing—but are nowhere to be found in Class B Reports. Is this because any mind generating a poltergeist must possess knowledge of how to create fire and writing? Or perhaps Bigfoot have found a way to harness the psychic effects of poltergeist phenomena to their own ends?
6. Any mixture of the above hypotheses.

The exact intersection of poltergeist phenomena and Class B Reports may never be revealed. For all we know, there may be no connection, or the link may indeed be as intimate as points 4 or 5 above. In some sense, it is entirely irrelevant—the important principle is to engage in critical thinking that challenges our preconceptions, forcing us to reexamine the paradigms we impose on objective data and ourselves. *To question everything.*

To look where the bullet holes aren't.

References:

Ellenberg, J. (2015). *How Not to Be Wrong: The Power of Mathematical Thinking.* New York, NY: Penguin Books.

Gordon, S. (2010). *Silent Invasion: The Pennsylvania UFO-Bigfoot Casebook.* R. Marsh (Ed.). Greensburg, PA: Stan Gordon Productions.

Kelleher, C.A. & Knapp, G. (2005). *Hunt for the Skinwalker: Science Confronts the Unexplained at a Remote Ranch.* New York, NY: Pocket Books.

Guiley, R.E. (2007). *The Encyclopedia of Ghosts and Spirits* (3rd ed). New York, NY: Facts on File, Inc. (Original work published 1992)

In fact, Celtic stories of the faerie folk share a great deal in common with modern Bigfoot lore. Despite their discrepancy in size, both allegedly frequent subterranean spaces; abduct children; are associated with ghost lights; are blamed for livestock deaths; braid horses' manes; are ascribed certain food taboos in indigenous culture; share similar odors; suckle milk from cattle; incapacitate or disorient witnesses at a distance; have close ties to the spirit world; and posses an intense interest in human sexuality.

Fahrenbach, W.H. (2005). Report #10928 (Class B): Hikers hear growl, wood knocking, have rock thrown at them. Retrieved December 1, 2017 from http://www.bfro.net/GDB/show_report.asp?id=10928

BFRO. (2017). BFRO Database History and Report Classification System. Retrieved November 29, 2017 from http://www.bfro.net/gdb/classify.asp#classification

Colombo, J.R. (2000). *Ghost Stories of Canada.* Toronto, CA: Dundurn Press.

Coleman, L. (2003). *Bigfoot! The True Story of Apes in America.* New York, NY: Paraview Pocket Books.

Healy, T. (2001, October 20). "High Strangeness" in Yowie Reports. In P. Cropper

(Ed.). *Myths & Monsters 2001 Conference Papers.* Paper

presented at Myths & Monsters 2001, Sydney, Australia (pp. 64-72).

Newkirk, G. (2016, December 8). Bigfoot is a Ghost: Interdimensional Sasquatch, The Green Flash, and Why We'll Never Find a Body. Retrieved December 1, 2017 from http://weekinweird.com/2016/12/08/bigfoot-is-a-ghost-interdimensional-sasquatch-tulpas-green-flash/

Godfrey, L.S. (2016). *Monsters Among Us: An Exploration of Otherworldly Bigfoots, Wolfmen, Portals, Phantoms, and Odd Phenomena.* New York, NY: Tarcher Penguin.

Coleman, L. (2008, November 14). Stone-Throwing Sasquatch or Poltergeist? Retrieved December 1, 2017 from http://cryptomundo.com/cryptozoo-news/stone-throwing/

Barackman, C. (2013). Why Don't You Look for Bigfoot During the Day? Retrieved December 1, 2017 from http://cliffbarackman.com/faqs/why-dont-you-look-for-bigfoot-during-the-day/

Swancer, B. (2016, September 23). Truly Strange Cases of People Kidnapped by Bigfoot. Retrieved September 5, 2017 from http://mysteriousuniverse.org/2016/09/truly-strange-cases-of-people-kidnapped-by-bigfoot/

Burns, J.W. (1954, December). "My Search for B.C.'s Giant Indians." Liberty Magazine, pp. 38-39.

Meldrum, J. (2006). *Sasquatch: Legend Meets Science.* New York, NY: Forge Books.

Bowers, C. (2014, May 29). The Unethical and Potential Dangers of Bigfoot Baiting: Part One. Retrieved December 1, 2017 from http://cryptomundo.com/bigfoot-report/the-unethical-and-potential-dangers-of-bigfoot-baiting/

Renner, T. (2017). *Bigfoot in Pennsylvania.* Charleston, SC: CreateSpace Independent Publishing Platform.

Bord, J., & Bord, C. (2006). *Bigfoot Casebook Updated: Sightings and Encounters from 1818 to 2004.* Enumclaw, WA: Pine Winds Press. (Original work published 1982)

D.K. (2013). Report #40534 (Class B): Strange encounter

experienced by LEO's camped near Goldbond. Retrieved December 1, 2017 from http://www.bfro.net/gdb/show_report.asp?id=40534

Monteith, R. (2013). Report #38923 (Class B): Possible nighttime activity in the retirement community The Villages. Retrieved December 1, 2017 from http://www.bfro.net/gdb/show_report.asp?id=38923

Healy, T., & Cropper, P. (2014). *Australian Poltergeist: The Stone-throwing Spook of Humpty Doo and Many Other Cases.* Sydney, AU: Strange Nation.

Violette, J.R. (2001). *The Extra-Dimensional Universe: Where the Paranormal Becomes the Normal.* Charlottesville, VA: Hampton Roads Publishing Company.

Clark, J. (2012). *Unexplained: Strange Sightings, Incredible Occurences, and Puzzling Physical Phenomena* (3rd ed). Canton, MI: Visible Ink Press. (Original work published 1993)

Megargle, A., & Megargle, J. (Producers), & Breedlove, S. (Director). (2015). *Minerva Monster* (Motion picture). United States of America: Small Town Monsters.

Wilson, C. (2010). *Poltergeist: A Classic Study in Destructive Hauntings.* Woodbury, MN: Llewellyn Publications.

Buckland, R. (2003). *The Fortune-telling Book: The Encyclopedia of Divination and Soothsaying.* Canton, MI: Visible Ink Press.

J.V. (2008). Report #24988 (Class B): Possible late evening incidents at a mountain home near Little Switzerland. Retrieved December 2, 2017 from http://www.bfro.net/gdb/show_report.asp?id=24988

Steiger, B. (2013). *Real Ghosts, Restless Spirits, and Haunted Places.* Canton, MI: Visible Ink Press.

Hitchings, S., & Clark, J. (2013). *Poltergeist Prince of London: The Remarkable True Story of the Battersea Poltergeist.* Stroud, UK: The History Press.

Bader, C.D., Baker, J.O., & Mencken, F.C. (2017). *Paranormal America: Ghost Encounters, UFO Sightings, Bigfoot Hunts, and Other Curiosities in Religion and Culture* (2nd ed). New York,

NY: New York University Press.

Matthews, D. (2016, September 6). Hear the Sierra Sounds, the Most Compelling Evidence of Bigfoot Speech Ever Recorded. Retrieved December 4, 2017 from http://weekinweird.com/2016/09/06/sierra-sounds-best-bigfoot-calls-ever-recorded/

Kallen, S.A. (2010). *Communication with the Dead.* San Diego, CA: ReferencePoint Press, Inc.

Josiffe, C. (2017). *Gef! The Strange Tale of an Extra-Special Talking Mongoose.* London, UK: Strange Attractor.

Holder, G. (2013). *Poltergeist Over Scotland.* Stroud, UK: History Press.

Pyle, R.M. (1995). *Where Bigfoot Walks: Crossing the Dark Divide.* New York, NY: Houghton Mifflin Company.

Wood, J.M. (1977).*Witchcraft and Superstitious Record in the South-Western District of Scotland.* Edinburgh, UK: Library of Alexandria.

Von Lossow, J. (2005). Report #12510 (Class B): Vocalizations near Scenic interrupt a camper's quiet evening. Retrieved December 4, 2017 from http://www.bfro.net/gdb/show_report.asp?id=12510

Bord, J., & Bord, C. (1989). *Unexplained Mysteries of the 20th Century.* Lincolnwood, IL: Contemporary Books.

Glanvil, J. (1689). *Sadiucismus Triumphatus: Full and Plain Evidence Concerning Witches and Apparitions.* London, UK: James Collins. (Original work published 1661)

Hall, W.J. (2014). *The World's Most Haunted House: The True Story of the Bridgeport Poltergeist on Lindley Street.* Pompton Plains, NJ: New Page Books.

Koch, K.E. (1986). *Occult ABC: Exposing Occult Practices and Ideologies.* Grand

Rapids, MI: Kregel Publications (Original work published 1978 as *Satan's Devices*)

Reles, R. (2014). Report #43648 (Class B): Memory told of possible activity while trapping in Horicon Marsh. Retrieved

December 4, 2017 from http://www.bfro.net/gdb/show_report.asp?id=43648

Hucklebridge, R. (2010). Report #27687 (Class B): Possible tracks found in snow and mud on family property many years ago near Lake Hughes. Retrieved December 4, 2017 from http://www.bfro.net/gdb/show_report.asp?id=27687

Burnette, T., & Riggs, R. (2014). *Bigfoot: Exploring the Myth & Discovering the Truth.* Woodbury, MN: Llewellyn Worldwide.

Courtney, S. (2010). Report #27692 (Class B): Mushroom hunter hears vocalizations and finds footprints near Jubilee College State Park. Retrieved December 4, 2017 from http://www.bfro.net/gdb/show_report.asp?id=27692

Cutchin, J. (2016). *The Brimstone Deceit.* San Antonio, TX: Anomalist Books.

Germer, W. (2017, October 13). SC EP368: Boy Scouts Encounter Sasquatch. Retrieved December 6, 2017 from https://sasquatchchronicles.com/sc-ep368-boy-scouts-encounter-sasquatch/

Noël, C. (2014). *Our Life with Bigfoot: Knowing Our Next of Kin at Habituation Sites* [Kindle edition]. US: CreateSpace Independent Publishing Platform.

Taylor, S. (2011). BFRO Report #29355 (Class B): Possible evidence collected after a woman is hit in the hand by a rock near Napavine. Retrieved December 6, 2017 from http://www.bfro.net/gdb/show_report.asp?id=29355

Adams, P., Underwood, P., & Brazil, E. (2009). *Borley Rectory Companion: The Complete Guide to 'The Most Haunted House in England.* Stroud, UK: The History Press.

Matthews, R., & Cawthorne, N. (2012). *Poltergeists and Other Hauntings.* London, UK: Arcturus Publishing.

Chestnut, D. (2014). *How to Clean Your Home of Ghosts & Spirits.* Woodbury, MN: Llewellyn Publications.

Bosch, D., Hajicek, D. (Writers), & Hajicek, D. (Director). (2007, November 7). Sasquatch Attack? [Television series episode]. In D. Hajicek & W. Yates (Producers), *MonsterQuest.* Minneapolis,

MN: Whitewolf Entertainment.

Ruickbie, L. (2013). *A Brief Guide to Ghost Hunting: How to Investigate Paranormal Activity from Spirits and Hauntings to Poltergeists.* London, UK: Constable & Robinson Ltd.

Redfern, N. (2013, August 6). Bigfoot and Electronic Intereference. Retrieved December 4, 2017 from http://mysteriousuniverse.org/2013/08/bigfoot-and-electronic-interference/

Bigfoot Crossroads [Screen name]. (2017, February 20). Bigfoot drains batteries! Bigfoot Outlaw Radio Ep31 Part 2. Retrieved December 4, 2017 from https://www.youtube.com/watch?time_continue=374&v=xy-UF8Xifzo

Germer, W. (2017, May 21). SC EP:326 The Quantum Bigfoot. Retrieved December 4, 2017 from https://sasquatchchronicles.com/sc-ep326-the-quantum-bigfoot/

Germer, W. (2016, February 3). Watch: Strange lights flying around. Retrieved December 6, 2017 from https://sasquatchchronicles.com/watch-strange-lights-flying-around/

Solomon, G, & Solomon, J. (2012). *The Scole Experiment: Scientific Evidence for Life After Death (New Updated Edition).* Waltham Abbey, UK: Campion Books. (Original work published 1999)

Hubbell, W. (1916). *The Great Amherst Mystery: A True Narrative of the Supernatural* (10th ed.). New York: Brentano's. (Original work published 1888)

Price, H. (2012). *Poltergeist Over England: Three Centuries of Mischievous Ghosts.* Devon, UK: F&W Media.

Hanks, M. (2016, July 29). "The Indians Without Fire": Stories of Sasquatch Over the Ages. Retrieved December 6, 2017 from http://mysteriousuniverse.org/2016/07/the-indians-without-fire-stories-of-sasquatch-over-the-ages/

Germer, W. (2017, November 19). SC EP381: Searching for the creatures. Retrieved December 7, 2017 from https://sasquatchchronicles.com/sc-ep381-searching-for-the-creatures/

Goldstuck, A. (2012). *The Ghost That Closed Down the Town.*

London, UK: Penguin Books.

Melton, J.G. (Ed.). (2001). *Encyclopedia of Occultism & Parapsychology: Volume 2 – A-Z* (5th ed). Farmington Hills, MI: Gale Group.

Redfern, N. (2012). *Wildman! The Monstrous and Mysterious Saga of the British Bigfoot.* C. Downes & J. Downes (Eds.). North Devon, UK: CFZ Publications.

Redfern, N. (2013, April 8). Sasquatch and a Ouija-board. Retreived December 7, 2017 from http://mysteriousuniverse.org/2013/04/sasquatch-and-a-ouija-board/

Briggs, K. (1976). *An Encyclopedia of Fairies: Hobgoblins, Brownies, Bogies, and Other Supernatural Creatures.* New York, NY: Pantheon Books.

Oklahoma's Boggy Creek

by Marvin Leeper

"Is that what yore a-learnin' my young-uns?"
~ Ma Kettle

Introduction

While the above *epigraph* quoted from an old Ma and Pa Kettle movie, might sound humorous, it nearly, very seriously, became an *epitaph* for my newly resurrected Folklore class at Murray State College in 2014. Nestled in the heart of the Bible belt, MSC's hometown of Tishomingo, Ok. (High school marching band, "The Pride of Little Dixie"), is the typical small southern town populated by Red State politics, fried foods and hardworking, God fearing people. Anything outside the perceived "norm" would be a hard sell, no doubt about it. The Folklore class had been on hiatus from the MSC catalog for nearly twenty years, when I hit on the idea to revive it; well aware the class had met its demise due to lack of enrollment (numbers to the Administration, interest to students), I was determined to design a class that would teach the basics of Folk study and be *fun* (insert gasps here) for the students. I asked a few students around campus and did some informal polling and what feedback I got was, in effect, "Who wants to read about Paul Bunyan or Johnny Appleseed?" I countered with additional queries such as, "What topics would you like to study if you had the choice?"

Now the rollercoaster ride was beginning. Topics ranged from buried treasure, outlaws, cry baby bridges, urban legends, stuff I can't mention here and, oh yeah…Bigfoot. I seriously considered giving up on the notion and then it came to me that surely there was some merit in all these stories. After all, Folklore can be seen as a cultural barometer, consisting of such varied disciplines as history, sociology, and anthropology. As I researched the *research* I found that, indeed, the tales of hairy wildmen not only had a historical precedent, there also existed three basic levels of folk study that, to my amazement, fit Bigfoot research like a glove…or perhaps, I should say, a shoe (think a super-sized Shaq shoe). Still there remained the problem of how to convince college Administrators and concerned parents that there was academic worth in including Bigfoot in the curriculum. The basic three forms of Folk study: oral tradition, material, and ritualistic paradigms each presented in Bigfoot research, so I decided to take the plunge. With the blessing of Department Chair, Prof. Jeana West, I promoted the course in the next semester's curricular catalog. Indeed, I was preparing to start a-learnin' their young-uns about Bigfoot and much more than I could have dreamed. During the course of my research for the class I would uncover a lengthy history of wood ape sightings along Oklahoma's Boggy Creek, read scholarly articles on waterway travel authored by noted naturalists, come to recognize notable behavioral traits of this cryptid creature and listen to and record countless stories. Oh those stories…

A Short History of the Region

Popular columnist and comedian Argus Hamilton used to write for the *Oklahoman* newspaper and always began his column with "Good morning Oklahoma and hello Little Dixie". For years this familiar and humorous introduction greeted Hamilton's readers who astutely got the joke. Simply put, Little Dixie was and remains a state within a state. Long noted for its strong identification with the Confederacy, this region remained one of the last to see an influx of out of state and foreign settlers. It's not that good old Southern hospitality wasn't prevalent in Little Dixie; it's just that, for years, you had to be a good old Southerner to enjoy it.

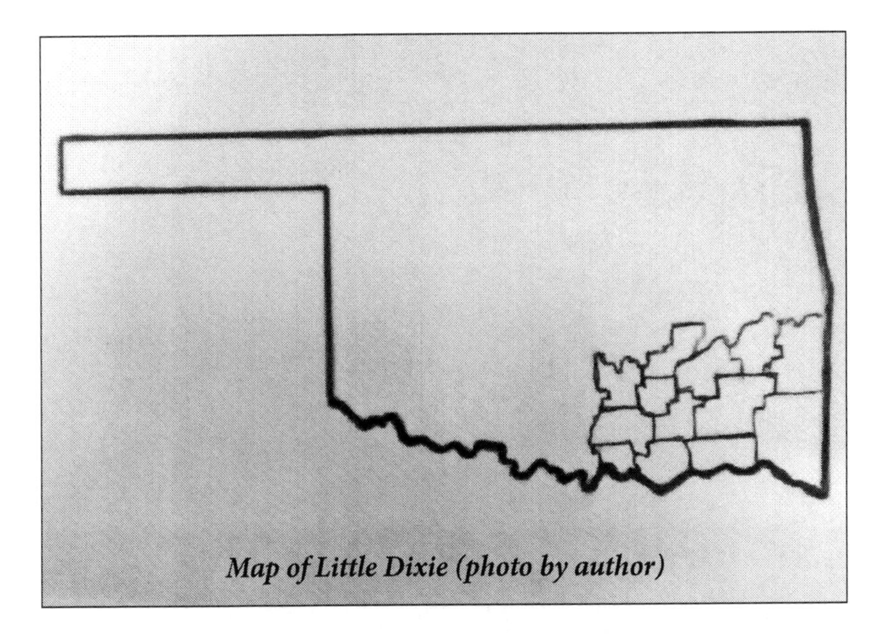

Map of Little Dixie (photo by author)

Indigenous Native American tribes, chiefly from the Caddoan Confederation, had maintained hunter/gatherer communities in the area since A.D. 900. As Hernando De Soto pushed farther inland, around 1592 he encountered settlements of Caddoan peoples along and either side of the Red River from that body's confluence with the Mississippi and Northwesterly to what is now Little Dixie. In pursuit of resources such as raw materials and, of course, gold, De Soto interacted with these inhabitants much as the Spaniards had when they first encountered the Aztecs. Spanish contact with the Native Americans of Southeastern Oklahoma, while not as drastic as that with the Aztecs, still took little consideration into account of the customs and traditions of the peaceful villagers that had settled the vast bottomlands and mountains (Caddo Nation, 2018).

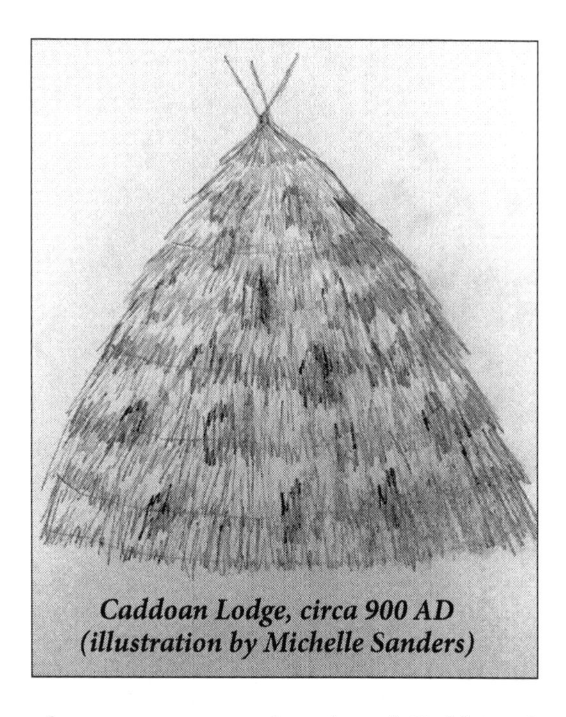
Caddoan Lodge, circa 900 AD (illustration by Michelle Sanders)

Among these customs are the tales of Caddaja, the Giant that taunted men and drew them into the forest never again to see the light of the day. While little elaboration was given these creatures by the Spaniards, similarities with the lore of other indigenous peoples lends a strong association with the creature known as Sasquatch or Bigfoot. Caddaja seems the most likely Caddoan candidate for being more Bigfoot like. Predating the Choctaw Shampe (in Oklahoma at least) by over two hundred and fifty years, this giant bears notable similarities, both in size and demeanor. Just as Shampe lived in the deep forest and is known for menacing hunters, so does his Caddoan counterpart. Caddaja took its malice one step farther though, by feasting on the flesh of human beings. Described in various ways (ogre-like, or even horned), Caddaja is most often represented as a hairy giant which is to be avoided at all costs.

One Caddoan tale tells of Caddaja's quest to kill and feed upon pregnant women. Similar to Shampe in size and attitude toward people, one is compelled to note the predatory nature of Caddaja, and its intended prey. To say that Caddaja is/was "cannibalistic" in nature, as has been alluded to by some researchers, would bear the connotation that the Caddo people themselves believed the creature to be human. Extent lore does not suggest any such kinship. Caddaja was seen as a monster that was to be shunned by the people at all costs; representing all that was seen as odious in their eyes (Native Languages, 2018).

Tales such as this one dominated the ancient history of what was to become Oklahoma well into the time of the French expansion into Oklahoma, circa 1719, when Jean-Baptiste Bernard de la Harpe traveled up the Red River to establish trade with the Indians. While the Spanish had sought resources and gold in the region, little commerce with native peoples had been established and by the early 18th century, their loose claim on the territory had diminished such that French fur traders, or *coureurs de bois,* enjoyed a lucrative exchange of goods and culture. This collaborative nature is evidenced by the establishment of the first white settlement, by Harpe, in Oklahoma at the site of an ancient Caddoan settlement. Le Flore County, which will figure prominently later in this chapter, was likewise named for a French trader (Oklahoma Historical Society, 2009).

France gained almost exclusive control of the region in the late 1660s and sought to increase the fur trade. The coureurs de bois set up rendezvous spots in far southeastern Oklahoma, including Boggy Depot in Atoka County, named for the nearby creek called *vaseus* (Clear Boggy) by the French for its murky or slimy waters and adjacent bottomlands. Commerce and relations gained such success that many Frenchmen took Native American wives and settled here permanently (Oklahoma Historical Society, 2009).

Shortly after the Louisiana Purchase, the Native American lands east of the Mississippi were confiscated and those tribes were relocated to what is now Oklahoma. The indigenous Caddoan tribes were moved to western Oklahoma. Relocating to Oklahoma along the Trail of Tears, the Five Civilized Tribes (Choctaw, Chickasaw, Cherokee, Creek and Seminole tribes) were uprooted from their homes and forced to travel to the west (Oklahoma Historical Society, 2009). The 1820s and 1830s were times of great change and upheaval for these people. Even in the face of seemingly insurmountable odds, the Choctaws kept up their spirits and retained their cultural traditions. In fact one might posit the oral tradition grew during this period as a new Bigfoot origin story emerged from the desperate trek to the Indian Territory.

More Native Lore and Leflore

Shamanistic and spiritual leaders still held influence with the tribe despite the White Christian religion that sought to dispel the ancient ways and replace them with the more European religions. In Tennessee, the Cumberland Presbyterians had ministered to and converted a large number of the Choctaw. But the white man's religion had not saved the Choctaw from relocation and many returned to the ways of old as they suffered on the Trail of Tears. It was here that Ohoyotubby, a Machiavellian shamanistic leader, began to gain notoriety. By appealing to those disenfranchised peoples, Ohoyotubby sought to gain as much trust as possible by any means available. Hushed rumors spread through lodges of the man whose very name meant "Woman Killer." In his power was said to be a beast man, seven or eight feet tall, built powerfully and swift as a deer. This animal tormented hunters such that the custom of leaving part of one's kill as an offering to the beast was taken up. Shampe, as the monster was named, was brought in captivity (it is not known if the animal was in physical captivity or under some spell) to the Indian Territory by Ohoyotubby (Hudson, 2011).

The Ohoyotubby scenario is the second origin story for a Bigfoot creature in Oklahoma. Originally, the Caddoans related that a similar creature existed here as early as 900 AD. Was the Ohoyotubby Shampe a totally different animal than Caddaja? Some skeptics say emphatically yes. These researchers claim that Caddaja was more of a spiritual entity than a physical presence. Some point to the varied descriptions of the animal as proof positive that Caddaja is not necessarily a *Bigfoot* creature but some other undocumented cryptid, however just as many accounts substantiate the Caddaja as a Bigfoot scenario. If we proceed with the hypothesis of Caddaja as Bigfoot then this creature was presumably in that geographical region prior to the first known archaeological discoveries of Caddoan culture dating back to 900 AD. These origin stories are relevant and important not only from the more accepted Folklore perspectives, but from that of the cryptozoologist as well.

Another of the precedent-setting tales from Little Dixie that alludes to wood ape lore is the story of Leflore and the Shampe. In an article published in the Oklahoma Humanities Council magazine, winter 2016 "Mystery Edition", I recounted the Leflore story and how it contains elements of traditional folk stories, as well as traditional Native American lore:

As the story goes, LeFlore was a giant of a man, noted for his bravery and generosity. The family farm was said to produce enough corn to feed half the Nation. LeFlore would often go into his barn and marvel at the cribs filled with golden maize. Then he noticed that his stores of corn were diminishing. He chose to ignore the trivial losses, thinking that the grain was spirited away by those less fortunate. Late one night, the dogs bayed at something in the barn and Leflore sped down in time to see a large man running away, arms brimming with his stolen prize. Leflore was surprised that someone that large could move so swiftly and effortlessly.

The next evening, he took up a position in the shadows, aiming to catch the thief. When he heard the barn door creak, LeFlore jumped out—and gasped. Rather than a starving man, he came face to face with Shampe, the hairy woodland dweller whispered about around the campfires of his youth. Emanating a foul pig-pen smell and towering above LeFlore's six-and-a-half-foot frame, the hair-covered abomination seemed hardly human. Springing into action, Leflore soundly swatted the top of the intruder's head with the flat of his hand. Staggering but not disabled, Shampe countered with an equally powerful stroke. Leflore, reeling from the blow, realized that here was a worthy opponent and, summoning all his strength, slapped Shampe atop the head once more. The conflict carried on for hours, each giving as good as he got. Bested in the end by the enormous Choctaw's endless reserve, Shampe slipped into the shadows, much shorter than before. (No doubt this tale is a bit embellished by the retelling over a century and a half.)

As one can see in the above tale, several critical components of the classic Folk tale exist: the hero is of unusually large stature, his opponent is equally large, and the task at hand is nearly insurmountable (Brunvand, 1998). First, Leflore is "a giant of a man" which is a common facet of all such folk tales both here and abroad, in that only a giant of a man could perform the super human feats the Folk hero is required to attempt. Next, he is pitted against a beast or beastly man that embodies characteristics, both in behavior and appearance that readily distinguish him from the pure or good hero. Finally, we note the comparison and contrast of Leflore's "generosity" and the beast man's cowardly thieving nature. Given the repetition of the tale and the number of years the story has been in circulation aberrations and or changes could have occurred. Taking this into consideration is a requirement for the Folklorist who wishes to ascertain any degree of validity of the account in question. Just as in the classroom game of whispering something in a child's ear then having him pass it to the next student and so on, distortions and alternate comprehension often change the semantics of the original dialogue.

The Leflore story bears up well in the subsequent camp-fire tellings I have been fortunate to attend. The basic storyline is well preserved and the motif of man vs. animal/beast-man remains intact. The corn being stolen by the Shampe holds a significant place in Native American life and Leflore's triumph in "battle" is majestic and ethically accountable. That the Choctaw's opponent is unusual and equally, or even more strong, is also important for being so equally matched. Leflore's victory could only have prevailed through his ultimate goodness, in effect, good triumphing over evil on a level playing field. Also in keeping with the Animal Tales and fables paradigm in which human/animal interaction usually ends in either an exchange of desirable traits or one side triumphing over the other for the betterment of that character's fellows, the tribe's corn is saved. In this case it is apparent Leflore has overcome the Shampe in an exhibition of physical strength and put an end to the theft of a valuable nutritional commodity (Brunvand, 1998). Taking into consideration the above mentioned criterion is good and well for Folklore, could there be any researchable merit to the legend? On the television program, *Bigfoot: the Definitive Guide,* noted primatologist, Anna Nekaris states that when conducting biological field research cataloging unknown animal species, the first method she utilizes is to contact indigenous peoples of the area for accounts of those mystery species in the local oral tradition and Folklore practices.

One must concede that conflicting reports on the appearance and characteristics of these creatures, especially within the same tribal boundaries do seem to lend credence to the scientific community's skeptical position. Can this argument be successfully countered? By referring to "Wood Knocks 2" for substantiation of the various appearances of Bigfoot like creatures, one can at least concede the possibility of validity in these tales. Beginning with the Caddoan Confederation's presence in Oklahoma in 900 AD, Caddaja has been present in one form or another. Jeff Stewart suggests creatures such as

Caddaja might have used the horns of animals to adorn themselves. To prove his point, Stewart asserts, horned Sasquatch-like creatures continue to present themselves even into today in and around the Denton, Tx. area. Dubbed the "Goat Man" by locals in the Denton and Ft. Worth area, descriptions seem to point toward a hair-covered, humanoid figure, more ape-like than goat, whether physically horned or sporting the horns of one of its kills (Weatherly, 2017). If this theory holds water as Stewart suggests, it would be worthy to note that Ft. Worth and Denton, TX are within the boundaries of the Caddoan Nation of antiquity.

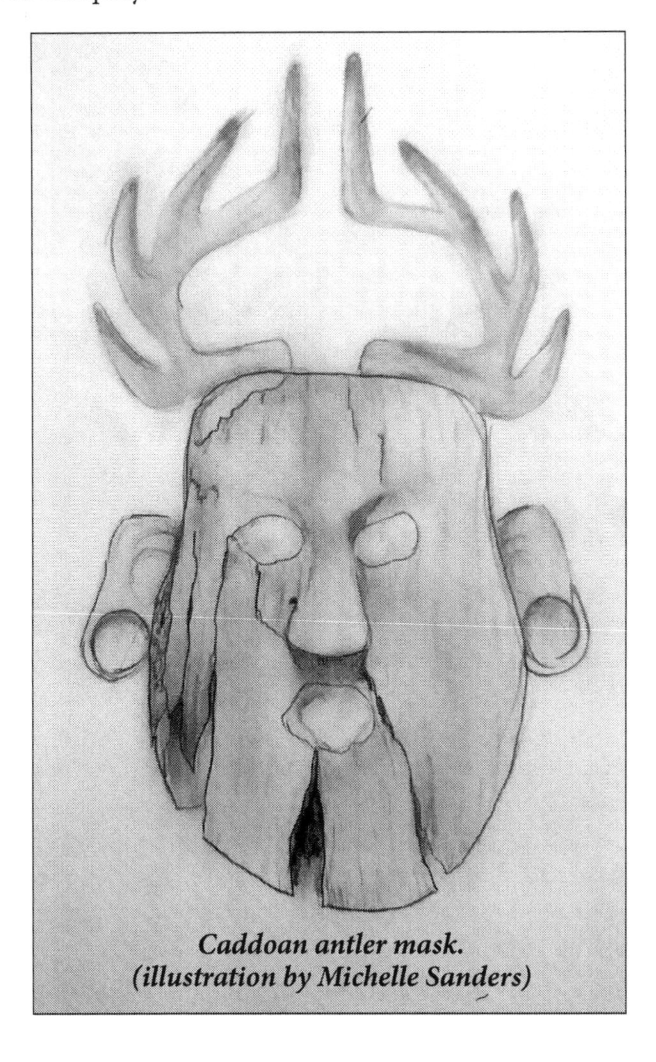

Caddoan antler mask.
(illustration by Michelle Sanders)

The sightings of horned Bigfoot-like creatures are not exclusive to the Denton, Tx. area. Across the Red River, the swampy and remote Randolph Bottom surrounds the Washita River, at the westernmost boundary of Little Dixie. Stories and tales of horned ape-like monsters have come out of this desolate and damp wilderness for over a hundred years. Dr. Derek Collins, a Tishomingo health care provider, first told me of the "Deer Man" of Randolph Bottom. Accordingly, the tale is as follows: sometime during the Great Depression the town of Russett was abandoned, and shortly afterward a record flood engulfed much of the community. People left by the droves and nature reclaimed the area. Sightings of the "Deer Man" began prior to the flood and continue to this day. In the 1970s, a railroad engineer had stopped the train on the tracks that bisects the Randolph swamp, and confided to a friend that a large animal loomed out of the dark swamp and rushed the tracks. The man vowed to never set foot out of the train again in that area. In my Folklore class of fall 2016, a student stated that her father and uncle had seen the monster, also alongside the rail road tracks. The creature carried a deer across its shoulders and the men were unable to tell if the antlers protruding above the creature's head were those of the deer or if the beast itself was horned.

If these accounts and rationale seem too speculative, one must take into consideration that primatologist Anna Nekaris does not seem to share the afore-mentioned scientific bias and bestows a good deal of credibility in these accounts via her initial contacts with local folklore and traditions (Bigfoot The Definitive Guide, 2011).

Whether creatures of Folk tales such as Caddaja and, to a lesser extent, Shampe existed outside the realm of legend remains to be proven. Perhaps science is correct and these mythical creatures have no place in the empirical world. If this is so, the accounts from other groups of people of non-Native American origin occurring prior to 1958 (the year the media coined the word "Bigfoot") should fall into the same category as any other Bigfoot sighting from the post 1958 era. A McCurtain County Oklahoma newspaper story from 1859 points toward just such an incident. Another such newspaper account from the same time frame carried reports of hairy Wildman stampeding cattle in nearby Pushmataha County (Arment, 2006).

The extent Folk tales in Little Dixie pre-date the supposed hinge date of 1958 is over *one thousand years* in the first case and nearly two centuries in the latter two. Here, the "media" as a sightings source argument erodes when considering it was the media itself that first perpetuated the notion nearly one hundred years prior. Unfortunately, the following tale, supposedly taking place in 1855, only adds to the debate.

Various internet sources touted "The Bigfoot-Human War of 1855" as proof positive that Bigfoot existed in Oklahoma prior to 1958. As the title suggests the "war" pre-dates Crew's find by more than a century. Briefly the story goes as follows: Members of the Tubbee and LeFlore families in Southeastern Oklahoma are law enforcement officers with the Choctaw Nation. A squad of thirty such "light horse policemen" is dispatched to the McCurtain County wilderness to apprehend a band of ruffians known to be raiding crops and stealing children. After a long and hot journey through the wilderness, the remaining eight (the trip was too much for the other twenty two) policemen encounter the band of "outlaws" only to find that they are, in fact, a tribe of Bigfoot-like creatures. In the ensuing battle, Captain LeFlore is beheaded by one of the savages and the creatures seem oblivious to the .50 caliber Sharpe's rifles the lawmen carried. The youngest of the Tubbee men realizes that the man-beasts can only be killed by shooting them in the head. After LeFlore's death and Tubbee's head-shot discovery, the law enforcement officers rally and destroy the creatures. Found among the carnage are the bones of nineteen children, presumably those of the missing children from the area. The authenticity of the event is brought into question and an examination is well handled resulting in a great deal of skepticism (Sasquatchhistory.wordpress.com, 2013).

Intrigued by the story, but certainly not convinced of its authenticity, I contacted the Choctaw Nation of Oklahoma and was referred to the Census Bureau. There I was directed to Gwen Takes Horse who proved as gracious as she was informative. Ms. Takes Horse offered her support for my scholastic research endeavor and suggested a perusal of Census information as an area in which to begin the search for authentication of the characters in the internet story. To her credit, she researched the 1850 through 1860 (and beyond) Choctaw Census records and found that, while all the names in the story proved legitimate, not a single one of these men were alive in 1855.

Similarly, in a presentation at the 2017 Texas Bigfoot Conference, David Weatherly gave a remarkably enlightening presentation citing a disturbing sense of sameness with this tale and another such incident concerning the tribes of the four corners region. Indeed, the entire tale seems to be lifted from the account proficiently provided by Weatherly and superimposed over the Bigfoot-Human War of 1855, rendering a sorry canvas of counterfeit "truth" constructed for consumption by the masses. The similarities were such that combined with my own research; a convincing argument can be mounted that the entire account is a fabrication, or a work of "fakelore," defined as "...imitation folklore attributed to a group that never had it" (Brunvand, 1998). In this case, at least, Folklore and history combine to out the hoax.

Oklahoma's Boggy Creek

There exists no shortage of sighting reports of man-like creatures in Little Dixie. A quick internet search reveals multiple encounters in most of the counties that make up the region. For the sake of brevity, perhaps no other area in the lowlands of Little Dixie has had such an impressive array of encounter accounts as Oklahoma's "Boggy Creek", Clear Boggy. Situated in the heart of Little Dixie, the creek winds its way to the confluence with Middle or Muddy Boggy before emptying into the Red River through five counties. Dropping fifteen feet from its fount to the confluence the stream is live year round, fed by numerous tributaries and springs. The mineral content is high and the entire area is a haven for wild hogs, deer and other game. Riddled as it is by countless creeks and streams, Oklahoma's Boggy Creek meets and even exceeds all the agreed upon criteria for excellent wood ape habitat.

Stories from the Great Depression in and Around Clear Boggy

It is safe to say that most sightings in modern times go unreported for reasons listed above. However, in less recent times when stories of mystery animals did not foster allegations of mental illness or outright breaches of truth, the public actually gave serious consideration to such accounts. One incident is still often repeated as factual in the Standing Rock community of Atoka County. Members of the family continue to live in the area nearly 90 or so years later, and have requested that they not be identified, such being the power of ostracization. I first heard the story when the actual witness' grandson brought up the subject in Sunday school back in the mid-1960s. I vividly remember the tale of a woman and her young daughter in the community who had experienced a terrifying ordeal one spring, many years prior.

Like most of the South, the Clear Boggy Creek area of Atoka County was an impoverished, agrarian society during the Great Depression. What separated this region of Oklahoma from the more urban areas was the Southeastern quadrant had always known belly gnawing poverty, initiating with the end of the Civil war and continuing into the present day. One old farmer facetiously said, "The Depression is over? Hell, we're so poor; I didn't even know there was one!"

Spring was an especially challenging time of year for the rural residents of the South. Stores of meats, both farm-raised and harvested from the woods, had been smoked and laid by and were running low. Home canned goods were likewise becoming depleted as the large farm families struggled to keep members fed. Dollars from cotton, corn and peanuts were similarly as scarce as sinners in Sunday school, and Little Dixie waged an age old battle against hunger. Poet T.S. Elliott proclaimed April the cruelest month but March was especially harsh in Little Dixie, and Elliott had never lived there. March was called "the Hungry Month" by old timers and Indians alike. April was weeks away from the life sustaining wild fruits and vegetables that had become a staple of nutrition in the region. Among such necessities were Polk Salat (I was fourteen years old when I learned this green was not a "salad"), dock and wild lettuce. These vegetables grow profusely in the bottom lands but were not yet in season.

For a couple of weeks, residents in the area had noted strange, guttural howls and moans coming up out of the Watson Creek bottoms in the Standing rock area of Atoka County. Watson is a tributary to Clear Boggy and is noted for its brushy swampy topographical features and provides habitat for ample wildlife. Mrs. Doe took to the banks of Watson Creek late one afternoon to supplement the evening meal with some of the few natural supplements available, a mess of wild onions.

With her that afternoon was her young pre-school age daughter, reckoned by a surviving brother to be about four years old. As the sinking sun relinquished the warmth of the day, Mrs. Doe was careful not to let the little girl get into the chilly waters of the creek. Back home the bean pot sat on the wood stove, awaiting the additional seasoning the onions would provide. Mrs. Doe knew she could not dally and placed the child up the bank on higher ground and away from the water's edge. Here the girl amused herself while her mother roamed up and down the banks searching for bunches of onions, all the while casting cautious glances in the direction of her daughter. As time was precious, the woman worked quickly and perhaps wished she had set out earlier on her harvest. Her thoughts were two-fold: gather an adequate amount of onions while keeping tabs on the child. Occupied with her multi-tasking, the family matriarch paid little attention to the opposite side of the creek bank. Usually, she would have been keen to any sights or sounds that might alert her to the presence of intruders or wild animals, but for the moment the work at hand and her young daughter had claimed her attention.

The child screamed one blood curdling scream after another. The panicked mother dropped her fork and bucket and ran immediately to the girl. Aware that during warm spring days such as this one, cottonmouth snakes came out to hunt and sun, she was fearful that her daughter had been bitten. Consumed with maternal instinct, she had not as yet looked behind her to the opposite bank of Watson creek. It was not until after determining the child was unharmed she looked in the direction the little girl kept pointing. Across the murky water she could not believe the incredible sight she observed. The woman's eyes transmitted a visual image to her brain that simply put, could not be processed. Crouching in a patch of wild onions, a huge black form rose from the bank to its full height, "bigger than any man that ever lived." Dropping a stick from its hand the creature grunted at the pair of terrified humans but made no effort to advance. Before the animal stood erect, Mrs. Doe had imagined it was a giant hog or even a bear. Now faced with the subsequent enormity of the creature's bulk and height, the woman's fight or flight impulse kicked in. Gathering the four year old in her arms, she bolted up the creek bank and ran as fast as she could toward the house, some quarter mile away.

In her terror she dared not look back. Sounds of snapping and popping brush accompanied by heavy footfalls kept her apprised of the beast's whereabouts. It was following her. As she ran she said she was faintly aware that the creature's footfalls did not sound as though it was likewise running, but rather ambulating at only a quickened pace. On more than one occasion while recounting the incident, Mrs. Doe was under the impression the thing could have easily overtaken her. (She always used the word "caught"). Not in a situation to ponder the animal's motivation for remaining behind, the woman continued to run until exhaustion finally set in and she resigned herself to the inevitable. Now weeping as was the child, she slowed her strides incrementally. Mother and child continued through the woods at a slower and slower pace, occasionally and as often as she could, mustering bursts of speed. The animal slowed its pace as well. Now she was certain the thing was toying with her and this awareness only served to increase her horror. What kind of thing would play cat and mouse with a woman and young child?

Making it to the clearing and home at last, she learned more of the strange creature's behavior. Bursting through the unlocked door, she dropped the whimpering child to the floor and frantically bolted the doors and barred all the windows of the flimsy saw mill slab house. The woman knew that at the animal's inclination, the doors or even the walls could be easily breached by the creature's massive strength. The game of cat and mouse continued. Twisting door knobs and all the while delivering heavy open handed slaps to the walls, the creature circled the house, occasionally pausing at a window to gaze inside, bending down to look through the top-most portion of the window pane. Mrs. Doe hid in a dark corner and clutched the child to her breast, comforting her and imploring the daughter to be silent. As the animal harassed the frightened pair inside it grunted like a hog and made what Mrs. Doe later compared to "monkey sounds." At some point, the terrified woman stated the creature would whine like a dog. The onslaught continued until dusk.

Arriving home from the fields just after dark, Mr. Doe found his wife and daughter barricaded inside their home. Recounting the afternoon's horror story, the frightened wife refused to stay there that night, so her husband hitched up the wagon and travelled up the road to the neighbor, loaded shotgun at his side. There the men talked of previous encounters with the "Wildman," and decided that come daylight they would hunt the creature down.

Assembling a group of men from the community, the hunting party returned to the shack at dawn and attempted to retrace Mrs. B's path. While tracking the creature, the men noticed occasionally branches had been broken and grassy areas depressed, but were perplexed when they found little else. Creek side they found some distorted footprints in the mud where the creature had crossed during its pursuit of the woman and child, but other than noting the unusually large size of the tracks, no discernible features were present. Losing sign, the hunters loosed the hounds which either were unable to catch the scent of the strange animal or were reluctant to take up the trail. As quickly as it appeared, the Wildman was gone.

Months passed and the family returned to normal, with the exception of the loaded shotgun always within Mr. B.'s reach and his wife's persistent habit of keeping the doors and windows locked. In autumn and spring alike, the strange wails, whistles and howls continued to emanate from the bottoms, but no one went down there to look for their source.

What separates The Onion Patch Incident from just another sighting report is that it raises some legitimate questions — if the events in the story are considered to be true. Why had the creature a stick in its hand while observing the woman and child? Though she couldn't be sure, Doe always had the impression that the animal was poking the stick into the ground. At first she passed the incident off as the sort of disjointed, surrealistic images often associated with remarkable, and seemingly unbelievable events, but later in life came to regard the stick poking as "monkey see-monkey do" behavior. (Here it would be well to note that Mrs. Doe's monkey comments came later in life, and it is reasonable to assume she knew less about monkeys and their behavior at the time of the incident.) This may be true, but is it not reasonable to conclude the creature was poking the stick into the ground for exactly the same reason Mrs. B. was poking the ground with her fork?

I was asked to be a speaker at the second Fouke, Arkansas Boggy Creek Conference in 2015. Between presentations, I was fortunate enough to spend most of the afternoon with Smokey Crabtree, to whom I'd been introduced a couple of years earlier by mutual friend, Jerry Hestand. While we visited, (Smokey's first wife was from a town not 40 miles from where I was raised), the topic turned to The Boggy Bottom Monster of Oklahoma. Smokey proceeded to tell me a tale about how the Fouke Monster was known to raid gardens and eat onions, "Bitin' the heads off of 'em and spittin' the greens out." I told him about the Onion Patch Incident and in Smokey's opinion, the Standing Rock creature was most definitely feeding from the same wild onion patch as was Atoka's Mrs. Doe. He went on to say, "They'll [the creatures] take a stick or a rock and use it to dig or pry somethin' open"

(Crabtree, 2015). If Crabtree's observations corroborate Doe's visual, then an entirely new element has been added to the conversation.

The author and Smokey Crabtree (photo by Jerry Hestand)

Tool use, while not uncommon in lesser primates does not require the critical thinking skills needed to facilitate *tool making.* As it turns out, one of the criteria for being human is described by philosophers in this way, "As far as we can discover only humans... *make* [emphasis added] tools" (Titus, Smith, and Nolan, 1995). While primates and some lower orders of animals may use tools, only humans manufacture them and tailor them to the task at hand. Beginning as a commonplace afternoon in the rural South some 88 years ago, The Onion Patch Incident continues to be the subject of study and debate nearly a century later.

About the same time of The Onion Patch Incident, downstream on Clear Boggy, future county commissioner Leroy Tigert drove his school bus over the old metal bridge every morning as dawn pinkened the eastern sky. Tigert, a quarter blood Choctaw, had heard the stories of the Boggy Bottom Wildman all his life and paid them little heed. It wasn't that Leroy didn't believe the stories (there was no reason not to believe them), it was just that he had never seen anything to prove or disprove the legends of the Wildman. That changed early one morning in the first spring of the Great Depression.

Tigert had begun his route before daybreak, as with every morning, and one of his young riders was excitingly telling of a "wildman" under the Boggy Bridge. As Tigert's route would take him back across the bridge on his trip back to school, the driver decided to appease the children who begged him to stop and look for the Wildman. Thinking that some indigent hermit had taken up residence under the bridge, Tigert saw no reason not to stop. At any rate, he might be able to help a poor destitute individual out by pointing him in the direction of food and work. As the school bus slowed to a stop atop the rickety, wooden floored bridge, the mists parted to reveal what Tigert thought was surely the biggest man he had ever seen. Children scrambled and piled to one side of the bus to get a better look at the hermit, who seemed to be clutching armfuls of rocks to his abdomen, Tigert quickly engaged the clutch and drove away with protesting children hastily regaining their seats as the old bus lurched forward. Tigert had not seen a man.

Covered from head to toe in brownish dirty hair; was what had to be the Boggy Bottom Monster. Forever fascinated by the encounter, Tigert let the town talk die down. Though he crossed the old Boggy Bridge countless times for the rest of his life he never once went down to search for what he had seen that morning. Recounting the story to only a few people over the ensuing years, Tigert was well aware that such an event could have a negative impact in so small a community. Some things were better left alone.

Most puzzling about this encounter was why the creature would have been carrying so many rocks in so peculiar a way. I contacted Tigert's grandson, Steve Stricklen just to check facts regarding the authenticity of the incident. Both of us had crossed Clear Boggy Bridge for years, but on this cold afternoon in January, we decided to journey to the actual spot and look around again. We reconstructed the event in our minds. If Mr. Tigert were heading to Caney after daylight, he would have been traveling roughly south. That meant the side of the bridge where the Wildman was seen would have had to be on Tigert's right or the west side of the bridge. We knew the area well from years of fishing but upon this excursion a decades old question was answered immediately. Surrounding us in the shallows of Clear Boggy were copious mussel shells; from a distance, the wet, dark shells looked exactly like rocks.

Steve Stricklen indicates the place where Leroy Tigert saw the monster in 1029 (photo by the author)

Had the Boggy Bottom Monster been gathering mussels in the early hours of that long ago morning? Perhaps. The area is still profuse with fresh water mussels and crawfish as the many fishermen that frequent the area can attest. If such an animal had the wherewithal to use a stick to harvest wild onions might it not be able to find adequate locations up or down stream for further nourishment? If animals such as raccoons could open the tough shells of the mussels for the food content inside, so too could an animal with a presumably opposable thumb. The Boggy Bottom Monster seemed to have forged a trail up and down Clear Boggy and its tributaries in its search for sustenance. What could be the animal's rationale for remaining close to water ways?

He Always Travels the Creeks

Having long ago pondered that same question, Daryl Colyer and Alton Higgins, Field Operations Director and Chairman of the Board, respectively, of the North American Wood Ape Conservancy, answered the query in a fact based and thought provoking paper entitled, "Wood Ape Sightings Correlations to Annual rainfall Totals, Waterways, Human Population Densities and black bear Habitat Zones" (woodape.org). These men bring years of experience and knowledge to the table and have no personal agendas to perpetuate their reputations. Here the two quite methodically studied the titular components to offer scientific data of why sightings of these creatures occur in specific areas. As to wood apes and waterway travel they posit, "Almost without exception, reported wood ape sightings occur near water" (Colyer and Higgins, 2012). Here can be seen a criteria of sorts to offer validation for wood ape sightings regardless of the time frame in which they occurred.

If most wood ape sightings do occur near waterways an examination of the two encounters listed above reveal that, indeed, waterways are present in each account, and as a matter of fact, Watson Creek is a direct tributary to Clear Boggy. If, by use of this validity measure, the Caddaja sightings and interactions with the Caddoan Confederation are to be taken into consideration as anything more than Folklore, a waterway should be likewise present. First to be scrutinized would be the location of the major village of the Caddoans circa 900AD. This village lay on the banks of the Red River, which was the main point of egress for Spanish explorers. Furthermore, Colyer and Higgins cite the Red River drainage Basin, to which Clear Boggy belongs, as a major source of sightings (2012). Later the French would travel the Red, Verdigris, and Arkansas rivers in eastern Oklahoma. These major riparian systems in Eastern and Southeastern Oklahoma are all noted to have an excess of greater than seventeen inches of annual rainfall. Colyer and Higgins point to venerated journalist John Green as the first to correctly observe that 80% of all footprint finds have occurred in just such areas (2012).

In addition to using waterways for travel, it seems logical wood apes would seek sustenance as would all mammals, near those same waterways. Usually a retiring and shy creature, the wood ape should quite naturally seek areas with abundant water supplies and low human population. The dense forests and woods of Southeastern Oklahoma easily provide enough anonymity for such a reclusive creature and, as most animals follow waterways as well, substantial food sources. In fact there are 65,000,000 acres of woodlands in the Ark-La-Tex-Okla area, literally spider webbing the map with streams, creeks and rivers (Colyer and Higgins, ill. 2, 2012).

Back to Standing Rock

As the wood ape seems to travel the creeks so do the hunters of Southeastern Oklahoma. Nearly every book about Bigfoot has its own collection of stories concerning a coon hunter and this chapter is no exception. When Mrs. Doe and her daughter had their encounter with the Boggy Bottom Monster, her son was not yet born. Now nearing 80 years of age he is still active and continues to hunt the bottom lands of his youth when he can. There was a period of time however, that such was not the case, "I'd always heard the story, you know, always heard the story about when it [the creature] got after Sis and my Mother, but, I never really thought a lot about it…it was so long ago and before I was even born that it just somehow didn't seem quite real to me." As a teenaged boy in the late 1950s the legend suddenly became all too real for him.

As with many a Saturday night in rural communities teenagers readied themselves for the much anticipated sojourn some fifteen miles into town. Hayrides and Fall carnivals were in full swing at the local schools. While those fortunate few readied themselves for the trip to town, less affluent youngsters amused themselves with sleepovers and night hunts. So it was with young Doe. Having been raised to hunt, both for sustenance and sport, the teenager lamented his misfortune at not being able to afford the drive-in movie that weekend, but sought solace in the thrill of the hunt. His father had raised two of the best Black and Tan coon hounds in the county and often let the boy and his friends take the dogs out on weekends. The night air was crisp and mist rose from the dark waters of the Clear Boggy Creek when the hounds bayed on the first cast. (A cast is the moment when the hounds are loosed.)

"At first we figured they [the dogs] had hit on a big cat or somethin.' They'd just run in circles and scent the ground and some of 'em would shake their heads like it was somethin' they'd never smelled before. None of 'em would take it [the scent] and most of 'em went back to the pick-up," he related (Doe, 2017). Being a life-long woodsman and partly out of juvenile bravado, the young hunter decided he would "jump" whatever the animal was out of the thicket the dogs had balked near. Upon cautiously entering the thicket the boy heard the sound of a large animal splashing into the cold waters of the creek just ahead. He further observed, "Now I know for a fact that water is shoulder deep in that part of the creek and this thing waded it like it no more than come up to its waist. You can tell the sounds water makes when a man is crossin' the creek and you can tell about how deep it is too."

At the head of the group the young hunter rushed to the edge of the bank in time to see a figure emerge on the other side. The carbide head lamp cast enough light on the shape for him to discern a generally human form but with a curious feature he could not quite make out. On the blackish/brown creature's side seemed to be an odd deformity or protrusion from the waistline extending above the shoulder. When the second member of his party, Buck Ables, arrived at the hunter's side, this young man had a powerful six-volt, hand held spotlight of the old metal type seldom seen today. One can but imagine the awe with which the two young men would have viewed a creature of this sort, but think of the shock and surrealistic effect of the scene they were about to witness...the creature had a young one balanced on its left hip. "It had a baby one on its hip just like a human mama would carry her baby. I'd intended to shoot it if it was that thing but when we seen that it had a baby on it, I just stood there with my mouth open. I sure never would've thought that," the hunter exclaimed. During the interview, one could see the junior Doe was reliving the moment. The sincerity and emotion with which he related the event still keep him rooted in the moment, and as he related, "It wasn't the last time I saw old 'Wild Thang'" (Doe, 2017).

A handful of weeks later, neighbor Ruth Graham, a school teacher, was coming home from a late afternoon visit with Mrs. Leora Ables when something incredible happened. As she topped the hill on the way home she caught sight of an enormous figure dashing across the road at the bottom of the hill. Thinking how large the person was she slowed her car for a better look, sure that the "man" would stop once he had gained the opposite side of the road. To her astonishment, the figure leaped across the ditch and lithely jumped the barbed wire fence on the other side. The creature disappearing into a persimmon thicket before she had the opportunity to make out any discernible features, Mrs. Graham decided the incident to be quite unbelievable and kept it to herself, for the time being.

For three or four nights the dogs had huddled on the porch. Mrs. Graham and her husband, Thomas, a Highway Department foreman, had initially thought coyotes were on the prowl, possibly a big cat, but it was uncharacteristic for the fearless canines to mass on the porch for several nights straight. One night in particular when the dogs were especially agitated, howling and barking at something just past the porch light's illumination; she mentioned her strange sighting to her husband. She was taken aback by his answer, "Ruth why do you think I told you to stay in the house after dark? I saw that thing with a baby on its hip going out the north door of the barn just before sun up about a month ago." Ruth and Thomas discussed what the teenage coon hunters had previously seen and quickly arrived at the conclusion the incident was no adolescent prank.

Now members of the Standing Rock community were on guard. Children were not permitted to leave their yards and roam the woods and creek bottoms as had been their habits. Livestock and pets were put up at night in an effort to keep the thing from preying upon them. Farmers, shotguns at their sides, hurried up their plowing to get home before dark and ranchers counted cattle every day. During those weeks and months pets disappeared anyway, especially dogs. What few hunters who had the courage to venture out at night reported game was scarce. While no one actually saw the Boggy Bottom Monster again during this time frame, occasionally a siren-like wail or a loud piercing screech could be heard coming out of the bottoms. Winter had come and gone and, apparently so had the monster. In the Standing Rock area it would be several years before anyone reported contact with the usually solitary Boggy Bottom Monster again.

While the happenings of the late 1920's Onion Patch Incident and Mr. Tigert's sighting along Clear Boggy are without a doubt, quite remarkable, the events of the late 1950s and early 1960s are much more so when the presence of an offspring is introduced. Obviously, all species must reproduce to remain viable and for that to occur there must be abundant habitat and sustenance. As Colyer and Higgins rightly observe, the riparian systems of Southeastern Oklahoma provide just such necessities in the hierarchy of needs. Given the time frame in which the two sightings of a creature with a juvenile occurred it is correct to deduce this would be the same creature and not two different subjects. Had the sightings happened years apart, one might assume the same creature to be multiparous, capable of producing multiple offspring, or perhaps more than one breeding female to be present. However, given the time frame and location it is safe to say the subject in these separate sighting incidents was the same individual. While it's a known fact large primates and even some primitive humans do not reproduce as often as those with adequate resources (in some cases as infrequently as four years between births for humans), researchers cannot factually estimate the fecundity rate or even the gestational period these animals might exhibit. Suffice to say adequate resources do present themselves so as to sustain a breeding population (as obviously evidenced by the testimony of two independent witnesses), but the question remains-how large is this population?

If the reports are true and there is a previously unknown primate of gigantic stature roaming the bottomlands and mountains of Southeastern Oklahoma, increasing human population numbers and diminishing availability of natural resources may account for the scarcity of sightings. No available fossil record of such a creature exists and the general public is ill informed as to the numbers of actual skeletal remains of any species found intact in forest lands. It is reasonable to assume few skeletal remains would be found even if these animals were extent in viable breeding populations. It then becomes incumbent on the few forward thinking researchers in the field to implement conservation measures to validate and protect the species all in the same fell swoop. Such is the lofty and daunting task that lies ahead.

The early 1970s were not without their share of serious monster activity and events of high strangeness in the Standing Rock area either. Mrs. Leora Ables, the friend whom Mrs. Graham had been visiting when she saw the animal cross the road, also had another relative who had seen the creature. When Buck Ables and T. Doe had seen the creature some twenty years before, Leora took heed to the young man's story. She knew only too well what had transpired at the Doe farm those many years ago, and though Bucky might be capable of a tall tale or two, she placed her trust in his account. She always cautioned her grandchildren about the creature and as her recently deceased husband had insisted, seldom went out after dark. It then came as no surprise when her adolescent granddaughter caught sight of the creature on a brightly lit autumn night in the mid-1970s.

Kenneth McIninch and friends had changed saddle blankets on their mules and headed into the bottoms coon hunting. Several of the saddle blankets had been left hung over the sides of the pickup to dry.

Hearing something prowling around in the back of her stepfather's truck, the girl opened the wooden door and screen to see an enormous figure standing at the end of the truck. The young lady could not tell just what this "man" was doing but she vividly recalls he had to stoop down to do it. When her mother asked why she had the door open the pre-teen answered, "There's a big old man prowling through the back of Daddy's truck." Thinking it to be one of the coon hunters returned to her husband's truck to fetch another saddle or some other piece of tack, the woman was more concerned with keeping the house warm and hurried to the door. At that moment the creature rummaging through the back of the truck turned its attention to the house. Mrs. McIninch became fully aware this was no "man" and quickly moving the girl aside, slammed and locked the door. The animal did not leave at once but stood for a time as if debating whether to approach the house or not. The two females moved away from the doors and windows and waited. After what must have seemed like an eternity, Mrs. McIninch peered out the window to see nothing. The creature had gone as quietly as it had come.

When they arrived back at the house the coon hunters had neither seen nor heard anything to indicate there had been an intruder, other than the displaced saddles, blankets and scuff marks in the gravel where something had stood next to the truck. Apparently the creature had devoted all its attention to those items recently used on the mules. Could there be a link to the mules and the creature?

In Southwest Coal County a rocky outcropping of granite, scrub brush, and cedar pushes upward to form what the locals call "Flag Pole" Mountain. While it is certainly not a true mountain its peaks hold as much mystery and lore as that of any mountain range. From Flag Pole Mountain it is said locals used to fly a huge white flag on one of the black jack trees to warn Southern sympathizers of the advance of Federal troops.

In sight of Flag Pole Mountain, on the outer edge of the Standing Rock community are the remains of the old White Hall church and cemetery. Populated until the 1960s by the descendants of Freedmen, White Hall has had more than its share of bizarre and unexplained activity. Though stories of darkly colored and hairy man-monsters haunting the area had been whispered for decades, it was not until the 1980s that one of the most incredible stories to date occurred. On the

Coal county side of White Hall Road, is a 660 acre ranch owned now by a family from Texas. Local resident, Jesse McIninch tells that back in the 1980s the ranch was owned locally, and the owner hired two young Mexican men to work the cattle and keep the fences up. The ranch was productive and the work was hard. The two cowboys slept in a mobile home near the feed shed and corral on the property.

For more than a few nights the two young men had heard unusual howls and hollers coming from the direction of Flag Pole Mountain. By the week's end the screams were much closer. Horses in the corral near the shed were wild eyed and snorting, their gaze fixed on a point of timber near the creek. The morning after a long sleepless night of dogs barking, strange cries from the feed shed and inexplicable banging, the two cow hands investigated the shed to find the door had been torn loose from its hinges and several sacks of grain torn open, their contents apparently consumed. Saddles and other gear had been displaced and thrown about. The horses remained in a panicked state. In their excitement, the men failed to look for foot prints, assuming the culprit was human, they instead looked for tire tracks, but noted that during the racket of the previous night neither had heard a motor. Taking up hammer, lumber, and nails the men boarded up the door and reinforced the windows and side boards. Taking no chances they were determined to catch the thief tonight or know the reason why.

The cowboys decided to stay up in shifts. The night passed uneventfully and the next day the pair dragged from their all-night vigil. As night approached they debated whether there was really any need to monitor the feed shed since after such extreme damage they doubted the culprit would return anyway. Still, just as a precaution, they moved the horses closer to the trailer. Staying up well after midnight, sleep overcame the cowboy on guard and he joined his friend in slumber.

The next morning at feeding time the two cowboys were astonished to find the door was once again forced open. More grain had been consumed and the saddles and tack were scattered around the interior of the building, with some even dragged outside. Nearer the trailer the horses had not made as much noise and even the dogs were suspiciously quiet. In fact the dogs were gone, returning a couple of days later.

By the time Mrs. Doe's son heard of the bizarre situation at the ranch, the cowboys had taken to carrying loaded rifles, secured in their saddle scabbards. Now in his forties, Doe Jr. had never forgotten his encounter with the Boggy Bottom Monster back in the late 1950s. Always the hunter, he decided to drive up to the ranch and talk to the cowboys about the strange incidents occurring there, and if possible set out after the creature. Upon arrival, the cow men made him welcome and the three exchanged stories about their respective encounters. Mr. Doe believed the boys and said he would do anything he could to help them catch or kill the mysterious creature. Leaving the pair to their own devices, he left for home with the promise to return in a few days. Over those next few days the cowboys would have quite an experience to tell.

The night after Doe visited the ranch the hands had their most harrowing encounter. Long about dark they began to hear the screams and cries coming from nearby Big Sandy Creek. Bracing themselves this time, rifles loaded and at the ready, the pair darkened the trailer and peered out at the feed shed down the hill toward the creek. The bend of the slope prevented them from a clear line of sight, and muffled some of the sounds that came up from the shed. The cow dogs, having returned earlier that day, were secured under the trailer and whimpered and barked at something the two men could not see or hear. One of the men decided to go out the back and try to flank the shed to ascertain if the thief was there. The dogs were more frenzied in their barking and had moved further back under the trailer. Now the horses had sensed something and began to become agitated. As the man opened the door to step out, rocks pelted the sheet metal trailer with such force that the aluminum siding was dimpled. The onslaught kept up most of the night. Just as the two men thought the bombardment was over it would begin anew. The next day, sure as the world, the feed shack had been ransacked, saddles and blankets scattered on the ground. What was it that urged the creature to plunder the saddle room night after night? The feed shed seemed a no brainer but the horse connection remained a mystery.

When Doe Jr. pulled up the next afternoon he was surprised to see the backhoe setting on the creek side of the feed shed, a huge pile of soil beside it. Wondering what the two men had been working on, he walked down to the shed to find a huge hole dug in front of the side door. The pit was about eight feet deep and, he estimated ten feet in diameter. Walking up to Mr. Doe the oldest cowboy asked, "What do you think of our trap?" Doe replied, "This hole is for that thing?" The younger man stated "Hell yeah." Doe simply replied, "You're gonna need a bigger hole." The pit trap didn't prove productive but the creature's harassment of the ranchers ceased after it was dug. It seemed the thing had figured out the cowboys were serious and moved on.

More Modern Boggy Bottom Monster Encounters

Sightings continued to trickle in from around the Clear Boggy Drainage Basin through the 1990s. The newspaper carried a story of a bear rummaging through a garbage can in the Wilson community. When the resident of the house turned on the back porch light the bear "stood up and ran away." Rather curious behavior for a bear and one might wonder if the witness was in error or the newspaper had misquoted her. Perhaps the dumpster diver was no bear at all. Accounts such as these populated most of the decade. It would be the early 2000s before more sensational and even chilling encounters were to come forth.

Much has been written about the high profile case involving the hoaxed bear skin suit used in Caney, Ok. in 2006. Needless to say the hoax dampened the true story of sightings by a local woman and her niece and nephew. Jerry Hestand has written about this incident and his investigation into it, and the ordeal can be read in "*Hunting Apes in America*," Hestand's excellently entertaining first book. Jerry also relates the encounters with a supposed white Bigfoot near Tushka, Ok. in some detail, a story that will be elaborated on in this section. Other less well known incidents in the area are as captivating as any from the Pacific Northwest, or any other location for that matter.

The following took place in 2007 only two miles or so from the location of the white wood ape sighting. A local farmer named Roy Rowton called me one evening and asked if I was still interested in cryptozoology. I answered that I was and he proceeded to ask me questions that told me something was afoot (I couldn't help myself). Anytime someone begins a conversation with, "You're going to think I'm crazy" my ears perk up and coming from this no-nonsense farmer I knew this would be something worth listening to. Rowton proceeded to question me about Bigfoot. What did they eat? How big were their tracks? Did the tracks look like a human's? On and on until I stopped him and asked point blank, "Roy is there something you want to tell me?" This was his cue. What followed was a torrent of personal experience that had been going on for nearly a month. It seemed to Rowton that the intense flooding had driven the creature up from Boggy Bottom to his and presumably other's farms. Bushel after bushel of yellow crook-neck squash, along with other vegetables disappeared nightly, and around the plowed edges of his field Rowton found tracks. Some prints reached 17 or 18 inches by his estimation. The impressions were deep in the ground and roughly in the same form of human footprints. I excitedly told him I would be there as quickly as I could, but he informed me the prints would be gone. So too would be the squash patch. Rowton had plowed the entire crop under. Astonished I asked him what had motivated him to destroy such evidence. Surely he must have been overwhelmed with fear, I thought. It was at this time the hard-nosed country spirit in Rowton came to the fore: "I ain't working my ass off to feed that woolly son of a bitch" (Rowton, 2007).

The next day I drove to the Rowton farm anyway. I was able to get a good description of the prints and Rowton fashioned a crude drawing of what they might have looked like. The farmer seemed utterly unafraid. His large frame silhouetted by the evening sun, he held a Remington 870 pump shotgun in his right hand as he gestured and described the field before it was plowed under. My investigation didn't turn up anything of worth other than that the nearby creek bed spider-webbed its way down into Boggy Bottom. The Bottom had yet to give up all her secrets. Little did Rowton know that only a few weeks earlier a very strange experience had played out for a young Tushka woman, just a couple of miles from the Squash Patch.

Ridicule and Ruses

Here, I must digress to point out that people who genuinely have an encounter with a supposedly mythological creature often have their belief systems shaken to the core. Such was the case with the lady who had the 2006 sighting Jerry Hestand wrote about in his book. When I attempted to contact her for this piece, I was told by her son that she no longer wished to comment on the ordeal in any capacity. He stated the subsequent hoax (involving the posed bear skin, or "Taxidermist's photo" as it is now called) had garnered his mother so much negative publicity that her health had become threatened and she had gone so far as to change her phone number and sever social ties. I immediately thought she was being harassed by enthusiastic Bigfoot researchers but was told in a matter of fact and to the point, "Its people in the community. They say either she's crazy or that she is making all this up. Who would make up stuff like that knowing it would cause them all this [expletive deleted]?" Similarly the young lady in the next story encountered a monster more terrifying than the one that emerged from the woods. Like Mr. Doe, whom we previously met, she asks that her name be withheld.

She has relocated to another town and changed jobs in an effort to escape the notoriety that her encounter created. When recently speaking of the incident with her parents I was met with outright denial by her father, "Naw that never happened, that was somebody else. I don't have no idea how they thought that was us." This account is also detailed in Hestand's book, *Hunting Apes in America* and is quite notable for two reasons. Just upstream a couple of miles from the Rowton farm, a large natural lake, lies between Boggy and the county road that bears the same name. Lain Lake is an overflow of Boggy and remains wet year round. Usually not over eight or ten feet deep the swampy recessed body spans twenty or so acres. A refuge for animals of all types, especially water fowl, Lain Lake is considered a sanctuary for hunters as well until the water rises. This season in particular, something emerged from the swollen swampy back waters that defied even the most indoctrinated Sasquatch investigator's experience.

The witnesses claim to have seen a Bigfoot like creature that was no larger than an average man. The creature was supposedly not even six feet tall, yet cleared a five foot crepe myrtle bush in a single bound. The most amazing thing about this animal, other than its diminished stature was the coloration. The animal seemed to be a dirty white color, perhaps gray, but certainly not the reddish brown or black hues most often reported. The family reported to Hestand that the torrential rains had strangled the country and closed many roads. Livestock was brought out of the bottom lands and moved to higher ground. Once again, it was the horses that alerted people something just was not right. Several days had past, and all the while the family's horses had been acting strangely, whinnying and running back and forth in the small corral, they seldom took their gaze off a small patch of timber a few yards away. When the source of their agitation was revealed the mother, her two children and the grandmother *saw the animal at the same time* (Hestand, 2017). Since the account is detailed in Hestand's book the focus of this report is on the creature's coloration, size and interaction with the horses, rather than the particulars of the case.

White or grey Bigfoot-like creatures, while not commonly reported are not all together unheard of. The North American Wood Ape Conservancy has had more than one account of an animal they have dubbed "Ol' Gray" in their ongoing expeditions in the wilderness of the Eastern Oklahoma's Ouachita Mountains. Author Jerry Hestand claims to have seen such an animal. (I know he saw the animal; I was there.) Finally, the Lake Worth Monster, one of the original "Goat Man" Bigfoot creatures, was also reported as white.

The small stature of the creature is curious but one would do well to remember that in the 1950s and 60s separate sightings revealed juvenile subjects alongside larger supposedly more mature creatures in the Standing Rock community. All these things, taken into consideration are interesting, but the point that stands out is that once again the creature is involved with horses.

Equine mane-braiding stories have been lifted from other lore (the mischievous Fae come to mind) and transplanted into that of the Sasquatch as obvious fake lore. Taking that piece of nonsense out of the equation, there does seem to exist some yet unknown connection between these creatures and their equine cousins. That connection does not appear to be amiable either. Recalling how the animal stood over the truck in Standing Rock and pawed at the saddles and still wet blankets back in the 1970s brings to mind the two cowboys just to the North on White Hall road and their 1980s encounter. The horses were terrified and the ranchers were concerned enough to re-locate their mounts closer to the house. The horses reacted to the presence of the unseen creature with extreme fear and panic. Do horses sense these creatures before other animals do? Why do horses react so violently when these beasts are near? Finally, why do these animals seem so preoccupied with horses? Only speculation exists instead of answers, but for those witnesses in the lonely Lain Lake area, the scars on their horse's abdomen speak to the sheer terror of the animal as it sought to escape the corral. Apparently in its bid to escape the animal in the timber grove, the horse had attempted to jump the fence and nearly impaled itself on the metal tee-post, inflicting serious injury in the process.

Half a dozen years later, an eerie event was about to take place. Michael Cottrell and his teenage son, Clayton had heard all the stories of the Boggy Bottom Monster and had taken it upon themselves to find the elusive beast. Backpacking alongside a creek south of Boggy Depot, they found a remote clearing on a long abandoned wagon road. Here the two set up their make-shift observation post and settled in. What seemed like hours passed and young Cottrell became bored and took out his cell phone. The elder Cottrell scolded the boy and made him put the phone away. Michael's rationale was simple; he figured the sounds and light from the cell phone would drive away any covertly lurking Sasquatch. To his horror, he was soon to learn just the opposite.

The longer the pair sat the more impatient the boy became. Michael knew patience would be of the utmost value on this endeavor and figured quietness and the cover of darkness would likewise be necessary. While Clayton fidgeted and played with the phone Michael's attention was drawn to the boy and not his surroundings. Only when the creature was twenty or so feet away did the man hear the swamp stalker. "It had been real quiet and then it sounded like real quick steps running up on me and then just stopped," Cottrell related. "I turned around and hit it [the source of the sounds] with my light and I just couldn't believe what I was seeing." Half hidden behind a sapling crouched an enormous reddish brown figure the "color of an orangutan." The motionless animal was wider than the sapling's branches but not as tall. "It was squatted down on the other side of the sapling like 'you don't see me'. Its arms were hanging at its sides but were still sticking out past the bush, and I'm like, 'You gotta be kidding me'. It's like the thing thought that if it was perfectly still I wouldn't see it. It was only about ten feet from us at that point" (Cottrell, 2017).

Cottrell states that he was in shock when he first saw the creature. His only emotion was that of total disbelief. Half frozen he simply turned around and collected his son and left. "I didn't run, I thought it might be like a bear and chase us if we ran so we just walked at a fast pace all the way out of the woods." Cottrell might not have run but he did look back, but there was nothing to be seen. It was as if the creature had been playing a malevolent game of tag with the two. Occasionally, Cottrell said he thought he could hear the animal following them but at no time did his light illuminate the reddish figure that had followed him. "I didn't get scared until I got home. Then I got to thinking about what that was thing intended to do" (Cottrell, 2017).

We were camped at Smith Park on the Sulphur River, near Fouke Arkansas during the second Fouke Monster Conference with several other presenters when Michael first publicly told his story. In camp that evening Lyle Blackburn and Robert Swain listened intently to Cottrell's story. Like me, they were fascinated by the account. While we each pondered the motivation behind the animal's behavior a general discussion developed following the comment that the two might nearly have been abducted. The group consensus was formed and we explored the possibility that perhaps the creature had used the light and noise from the cell phone, and the fact that Michael's attention was focused on the boy to its advantage. Whatever the creature's motivation might have been the incident left Cottrell in a state such that he doubted what he saw. For quite some time the man questioned if what he saw was reality or the product of his own mind. Two years later he would have an answer.

A Bigfoot in Little Dixie

Driving home from a rendezvous with other Sasquatch enthusiasts, Cottrell decided to detour to an area not far from Boggy Depot. As he drove down the desolate dirt roads he intently eyed the roadsides for any signs of the creature he had seen that night south of Boggy Depot. Not really expecting to see anything, Michael let his mind wander back to the past event, and when his headlights illuminated a pair of greenish eyes in the ditch to his right, he thought little about it. When the light from his head lamps was bright enough for him to make out the terrain in which the illuminated eyes shone, he realized that whatever he was seeing was large, extremely large. Bounding across the small creek to his right and up the bank and across the road was an astounding thing that moved with the swiftness of a deer but whose eyes must have towered seven or eight feet above the ground. The body was an outlined blur, so fast was the animal. Cottrell speeded up to the point where the thing had crossed the road and got out to look for sign. No tracks or imprints were visible on the roadway or the area into which the beast had dropped out of sight. Searching in the creek on the opposite side of the road, Cottrell could barely see some sign of scuff marks in the creek bed. Not wanting to tempt fate the researcher marked the spot on his GPS and headed home for some badly needed sleep.

Returning the next day with a friend, Michael immediately entered the creek bed and found three impressions. The first on the west side of the creek was little more than a scuff mark in which toe prints were barely discernible. The mud and clay of the creek bank had not cooperated in producing easily recognizable prints. Across the creek on the east side was a long five-rowed scratch mark probably five or six inches across. Cottrell could easily read the situation and determined the animal had made this mark with its foot while coming out of the creek. However easily one might reconstruct the incident from these impressions if onsite, neither had the easily recognizable traits that would make one say, "That's a foot print." Somewhat despondent, the researcher continued his task, contemplating what would be the best way to measure from one impression to the other to get some idea of the stride of this animal. Stepping into the soft damp soil of the creek bed it occurred to him there was no way anything could have stepped from the west side of the creek to the upper bank of the east side unless it was insanely large. Though unusually elevated, the height of the eyes he witnessed the night before had not given him such an immense sense of size.

While surveying the cattle tracks in the creek bed, Cottrell's misgivings were well founded. Almost precisely in the middle of the creek was a large print partly obscured by the cattle tracks it nestled in. The print, while lacking good five toe definition was easily recognizable and Cottrell muttered aloud, "That's a Bigfoot print." After careful examination he and his friend cast the track using plaster of Paris. Admittedly not the best track cast, the print is not ambiguous in the least as to what it is and examination by several wood ape researchers confirm that it is most likely that of a wood ape.

Michael Cottrell displays his track cast (photo by the author)

The print measured 14 inches long and over five inches wide at the ball of the foot. Cottrell's doubts had been put to rest and the incident in Boggy Depot had come full circle. "I felt some vindication with this sighting and track find. I didn't have my son's safety to think about and I went for it. This is what I found," he proclaims. "As far as those who don't believe, I don't mind. I'm not sure I would believe me either if it hadn't happened," he asserts with a grin (Cottrell, 2017). Cottrell's was not the last mysterious footprint found in the area.

In January of 2015, truck driver Dale Baughman delivered a load of gravel to the ranch where the two cowboys had their bizarre encounter. The ranch owner, his son and father were camped in an RV at the spacious lake on the property, and the Texas man reluctantly approached Baughman with a very strange question. Baughman recalls that somehow the topic of Bigfoot was broached and the rancher asked if he believed such a creature existed. Baughman replied that he was somewhat skeptical yet open-minded regarding the animal. At that time the rancher told Baughman of the encounter the two ranch hands had in the 1980s. The trucker confirmed he was aware of the accounts and this seemed to alleviate the Texan's concern. It was then that he broke the story to Baughman of what had just occurred that morning.

Just after daybreak the three men were observing bald eagles fishing on the lake when the eldest man spotted movement down the dam. Turning his attention to a spot where the woods thinned and a clearing started, the older gentleman was shocked to see a huge brown figure emerge. Gaining the attention of the other men, he exclaimed, "It's a damn Bigfoot!" When the others looked, they all agreed. At first the thing walked rather leisurely and when it became aware of the men high on the dam, picked up its pace. The animal never broke into a run but nevertheless moved with amazing rapidity. Baughman recalls that the men stated that the movement of the creature was fluid and graceful. While it seemed to stride effortlessly, the men were amazed that it "…walked as fast as a rabbit runs" (Baughman, 2015).

The Texans had made a halfhearted search of the area but had found little in the way of physical evidence. Satisfied with the dirt work, they packed up and headed home later that afternoon. Baughman obtained permission to come back to the property and did so the next day. At the end of the dam where he had dumped the gravel he began an examination of the area and to his astonishment found several tracks around the fresh gravel pile. One of these he cast as best he could. The others he simply left alone as these were not of the quality of what he had cast. His skepticism challenged by the track find, the trucker now considers wood apes a possibility. Still not a true "believer," Baughman notes that he always carries a shotgun in the dump truck now "…just in case" (Baughman, 2017).

Michael Cottrell displays his track cast (photo by the author)

40 Years in the Making

In February of 1976, a friend of mine and I were cruising the remote backroads near Caney, Ok. As was our custom on these late night adventures we stopped on the old Boggy Bridge. Shining our head lamps into the icy waters below we could have never been prepared for the events the next few minutes afforded us. As my friend shone his light in the thick understory at the southeast end of the bridge, the woods erupted in a fury of strange and malevolent sounds, and the trees absolutely shook with fury. Rocks and branches flew in our direction from the brush and it seemed as if some demonic thing was bent on our destruction. The tree limbs breaking and shaking were high enough from the ground that we thought a large animal was up in the branches. Screeches, screams and whistles assaulted our ears, and dumbfounded we could but stand frozen and silent. As suddenly as the din had begun the source moved rather rapidly downstream still screaming and throwing things into the water in an ambulatory fit of rage. When it was all over we turned to each other and the first word out of my buddy's mouth was, "Monkey."

Indeed our unseen assailant sounded like nothing comparable save an enraged chimpanzee. The rock and limb throwing was utterly beyond our experience and we stayed on the frozen bridge, shivering with adrenaline for hours. The animal never returned that night, and, to my knowledge did not for forty years.

John Hairell at the location of the 29 foot trackway (photo by the author)

The North American Wood Ape Conservancy published John Hairell's report on the 29 foot trackway found on May 6, 2016 just days after it occurred (woodape.org). We had been driving the backroads with a new dash cam I had just installed, when I recounted the events of forty years prior to John. As we neared the area we decided to go back to the old bridge on a lark. As we pulled off the road and up to Boggy, we never really thought the events following would ever come to fruition. Exiting the truck, I distinctly remember telling John, "I always like to check all the trails before we even get to the creek bank." Hairell nodded in the affirmative and set out, head down and intently scanning the wet ground, headlamp on. Remarkably he'd not gone thirty yards when he said rather intently, "Marv…come here."

I hurried over to see his discovery and before us lay a line of unusual footprints in single file that stretched from our position to over the edge of the creek bank. Neither of us wanted to jump to conclusions, but the anatomy of these prints was much more bulky and thick than that of a typical human footprint. Though the tracks measured only just over a foot in length, the width and overall dimensions spoke of their maker as *massive.* From heel to toe the steps measured an average of thirty six to thirty eight inches, making the overall stride seventy two to seventy six inches. Hairell, who is over six feet one, could not replicate the distance between prints without losing his balance.

No one has been able to reproduce a similar trackway in the peculiar single file fashion. In total there were nine prints in the trackway which spanned a distance of at least twenty nine feet. The best of the prints was measured and photographed and appears here. The tracks stretched from the wet clay of the creek bank to a fence where they apparently disappeared into a grassy field. Presumably their maker had crossed the fence and blended into the timber. Had we finally found physical evidence of the mysterious animal I first encountered on this very site forty years earlier? Or were we the victims of a hoax? For four decades the question has been imbedded in my mind: "What the hell happened that night?"

John Hairell measures the 29 foot trackway (photo by the author)

The best of the nine prints found in the 29 foot trackway (photo by the author)

The question still looms large some year and a half after the trackway find. Assuming these prints are valid only underscores my curiosity. All the centuries old Folk tales I've heard, all the scholarly papers I've read and all the accounts I've recorded only serve to open my mind to the possibilities of the mysteries that surround us. The fateful day I accepted the challenge to revive the Folklore curriculum and design a class fun and informative for the kids, I had no clue that I was to become a student as well. Oklahoma's Boggy Creek guards her secrets like a June Bride. Perhaps one day organizations such as the North American Wood Ape Conservancy will supply science with the necessary criteria for validation of the species. Until that day comes we still have the stories. Oh those stories…

Contributor Biographies

Bruce Champagne

Bruce Champagne has been involved with the investigation of relict hominoids and other cryptids for over forty years, and has been published in the Journal of Cryptozoology, International Cryptozoology Journal, and Elementum Bestia and Dracontology journals. Bruce has also written cryptozoology-related magazine articles, appeared in television and radio programming, and provided background information and consultation for other programming and projects. Bruce has been invited to speak at international functions, and his research is widely cited.

Bruce is the Director of Cryptozoology Research for the Unexplained Utah group, is a member of the International Cryptozoology Society and British Columbia Scientific Cryptozoology Club, and was a member of the original International Society of Cryptozoology. He can be contacted at brucechampagne.com.

Joshua Cutchin

Joshua Cutchin is a North Carolina native with a longstanding interest in Forteana. He holds a Masters in Music Literature and a Masters in Journalism from the University of Georgia, and currently resides in Roswell, Georgia. He is the author of two books: 2015's "A Trojan Feast: The Food and Drink Offerings of Aliens, Faeries, and 2016's "The Brimstone Deceit: An In-Depth Examination of Supernatural Scents, Otherworldly Odors, & Monstrous Miasmas." Both are published by Anomalist Books. Joshua is also a contributor to Robbie Graham's 2017 collection of ufological essays "UFOs: Reframing the Debate."

Cutchin is also a published composer and maintains an active performing schedule as a jazz and rock tuba player, having appeared on eight albums and live concert DVDs. Joshua has appeared on a variety of paranormal programs discussing his work, including Coast to Coast AM, Mysterious Universe, Binnall of America, and The Gralien Report. He can be heard on the weekly podcast Where Did the Road Go? and maintains an online presence at:

www.JoshuaCutchin.com

Marvin Leeper

Marvin Leeper teaches English Composition and Folklore at Murray State College in Tishomongo, Ok. Leeper designed the course curriculum for MSC's first philosophy class.

He is a 32nd degree Scottish Rite Mason and an official in Tishomingo Lodge #91. He is actively involved in Masonic and Templar research.

His life-long fascination with cryptid creatures began in childhood and continues to this day, culminating in the discovery of a 29 foot long track way on the Clear Boggy Creek in Atoka, Ok.

Leeper has given presentations and/or acted as host of the Honobia Bigfoot Festival story telling on numerous occasions over the last 5 years. He is an Expedition team leader into the wilderness of the Ouachita mountains for the North American Wood Ape Conservancy.

Among numerous academic papers, his work can be seen in *Monster Memories and the Oklahoma Humanities Council Journal.* He is currently at work on a paper entitled, "Little: Cultural Syncretic Similarities of the Choctaw Little People and the Irish Leprechaun".

Nick Redfern

Nick Redfern is the author of numerous books on UFOs, lake-monsters, the Roswell UFO crash, zombies and Hollywood scandal, including *Men in Black; Chupacabra Road Trip; The Bigfoot Book; and Close Encounters of the Fatal Kind.*

Nick has appeared on many TV shows, including Fox News; the BBC's Out of this World; the SyFy Channel's Proof Positive; the History Channel's Monster Quest, America's Book of Secrets, Ancient Aliens and UFO Hunters; the National Geographic Channel's Paranatural; and MSNBC's Countdown with Keith Olbermann.

He can be contacted through his blog at:

http://nickredfernfortean.blogspot.com

Timothy Renner

Timothy Renner is an Illustrator, author, and folk musician living in Pennsylvania. His illustrations have appeared in the pages of various books, magazines, fanzines and comics as well as on many record and CD covers. Since 1995, Timothy has been making music both solo and with his band, Stone Breath. Stone Breath has released over a dozen albums. Timothy is the creator of "Strange Familiars," a podcast concerning the paranormal, weird history, folklore and the occult. He makes regular appearances on the paranormal radio show, "Where Did the Road Go?," and has appeared as a guest on many other podcasts and radio programs, including "Coast to Coast AM."

Find Timothy at:

www.StrangeFamiliars.com

Robert Robinson

Robert Robinson was born at Hamilton AFB, CA. He grew up an Army brat and had the privilege of visiting numerous countries during his childhood. Robert enlisted in the United States Army in June 1982 and served for 21 years. He retired in 2003 and started teaching JROTC at Summerlin Academy in Bartow, Florida. Rob has a Bachelor's Degree in Criminal Justice from Everest University and an Associate's Degree in General Studies from the Central Texas Collage and is certified PADI wreck diver.

Robert became interested in Cryptozoology after watching the movie "Legend of Boggy Creek" and the television series "In Search Of." Because the whole subject of real monsters scared him, Rob started researching the subject by reading every book he could find on cryptozoology. The fear turned into intrigue and later turned into a passion and hobby. Robert first legend trip was investigating MoMo, the Missouri monster. Rob has filmed segments on the Florida Skunk Ape for PBS's "Weird Florida: On the Road Again", "Monsters and Mysteries of America" and "Bigfoot in America" on Destination America channel. Along with Bigfoot and other cryptids, Robert and his wife Tracy also investigates haunted places, UFO, buried treasure and mysterious places.

Robert has written for numerous magazines including Cryptid Culture and World Explorers magazine. Robert's book "Legend

Tripping: The Ultimate Adventure" was published in 2016.

Find Robert online at:

http://legendtrippersofamerica.blogspot.com/

Sam Shearon

Cover artist Sam Shearon is an English dark artist born in Liverpool, England. Specializing in horror and science-fiction, his work often includes elements inspired by vintage tales of monsters and madmen, dark futures, post-apocalyptic genres and classic literature including H.P.Lovecraft's The Call of Cthulhu, Oscar Wilde's The Picture of Dorian Gray and the modern classics Clive Barker's Hellraiser and the Books of Blood all of which he has fully illustrated.

Shearon's main influences stem from ancient cultures, the occult, industrial/art/revolution-eras, the supernatural, the paranormal, cryptozoology and the unexplained. Shearon has created covers for comic books and graphic novels including Clive Barker's HELLRAISER, The X-Files, Mars Attacks, 30 Days of Night, Angel, KISS, and more.

He has created album art and merchandise designs for some of the biggest names in rock music including Iron Maiden, Rob Zombie and Godhead.

Shearon studied at the University of Leeds in the College of Art & Design, West Yorkshire, England. He was awarded a Bachelor of Arts Degree with Honors in 2000 for Visual Communication. Shortly after, he went on to become a qualified Art teacher gaining a Post-Graduate Certificate in Education from Huddersfield University. His first solo exhibition entitled "A Walk on the Darkside" in 2003, featured forty-five pieces of his original artwork including 6-foot-tall (1.8 m) demonic statues, biomechanical monsters and giant canvases depicting images of horror and the macabre. The exhibition was featured in various national newspapers including The Daily Telegraph as well as BBC Radio One and live interviews on BBC Radio Leeds North. The show attracted protests and boycotts over its inclusion of animal bones, and the mutilation and disembowelment of children's toys, but the show was extended to six weeks due to popular demand.

His work has been described by the British press as "bizarre," "grotesque," "gruesome," and "groundbreaking." Shearon is known for his work in the field of cryptozoology, most notably for compiling artists impressions, of the Beast of Lytham from eyewitness accounts. Shearon's cryptozoological art was on display at the 2005 Weird Weekend, an annual conference at the Centre for Fortean Zoology. His work can be found in publications of the Fortean Times, Paranormal Magazine and other cryptozoology and paranormal publications.

http://www.mister-sam.com

Arbra Dale Triplett

Arbra Dale Triplett is an author, journalist, copywriter, veteran and editor. He's been writing fiction, advertising, marketing and UFO-related content for more than twenty-five years. Born in Springfield, Missouri to an Air Force family, he grew up in Texas, Colorado and Illinois before spending thirteen years in Germany. He studied English and History at Oklahoma Christian University, Harding University and Lubbock Christian. He served abroad in the Marine Corps for 4 years, drove semi trucks from coast to coast hauling anything from live bees to oversized freight, and flew in the Air Force as a Loadmaster on a C-130 cargo transport. He's hung his hat from Alaska to Florida and a lot of places in between. He has had a life long fascination with the unexplained, and has a soft spot for those who seek the truth. He is the author of Halcyon's Wake: Faith, and Benjamin Oliver Flanagan. His edited works include Paternus, by Dark Ashton; Strange Intruders, Men In Black, Haunted Toys, Wood Knocks, My Haunted Journal, with David Weatherly and Ross Allison; and Hunting Apes in America by Jerry Hestand. He makes his home on Table Rock Lake in the Missouri Ozarks. Need an editor for your own works? Then reach out to Dale on Twitter @DaleTriplett or on Facebook.

David Weatherly

David Weatherly is a renaissance man of the strange and supernatural. He has traveled the world in pursuit of ghosts, cryptids, UFOs, magic, and more. From the specters of dusty castles, to remote, haunted islands, from ancient sites, to modern mysteries, he has journeyed to the most unusual places on the globe seeking the unknown.

David became fascinated with the paranormal at a young age. Ghost stories and accounts of weird creatures and UFOs led him to discover many of his early influences. Writers such as such as John Keel, Jacques Vallee, Hans Holzer and others set him on course to spend his life exploring and investigating the unexplained.

Throughout his life, he's also delved into shamanic and magical traditions from around the world, spending time with elders from numerous cultures in Europe, the Americas, Africa and Asia. He has studied with Taoist masters in China, Tibetan Lamas, and other mystics from the far east. He's picked up knowledge from African and Native American tribal elders and sat around fires with shaman from countless other traditions.

Along his path, David has also gathered a lot of arcane knowledge, studying a range of ancient arts from palmistry, the runes, and other obscure forms of divination, to alchemy and magick. He has studied and taught Qigong and Ninjutsu, as well as various energy related arts.

David has also studied stage and performance magic.

His shamanic and magical background has given him a unique perspective in his explorations into the unknown, and he continues to write, travel and explore, leaving no stone unturned in his quest for the strange and unusual.

David has investigated, and written about, a diverse range of topics including, Hauntings & Ghosts, Cryptozoology, Ufology, Ancient Mysteries, Shamanism, Magic and Psychic Phenomena.

In 2012, David founded the independent media and publishing company, Leprechaun Productions.

He has been a featured speaker at conferences around the world and has lectured for countless paranormal and spiritual groups.

He is a frequent guest on Coast to Coast AM with George Noory, Spaced Out Radio and other radio programs. David has also appeared on numerous television shows including the Travel Channel's Mysteries of the Outdoors, History Channel's Ancient Aliens, Beyond Belief and other programs.

David's books include Strange Intruders, Black Eyed Children and the "Haunted" series.

To find David online:

http://twocrowsparanormal.blogspot.com/

http://www.leprechaunpress.com/

Made in the USA
Middletown, DE
14 June 2018